Felix Adler

American Liberal Religious Thought

Donald A. Crosby & W. Creighton Peden
General Editors

Vol. 5

PETER LANG
New York • Washington, D.C./Baltimore • Boston
Bern • Frankfurt am Main • Berlin • Vienna • Paris

Howard B. Radest

Felix Adler

An Ethical Culture

PETER LANG
New York • Washington, D.C./Baltimore • Boston
Bern • Frankfurt am Main • Berlin • Vienna • Paris

Library of Congress Cataloging-in-Publication Data

Radest, Howard B.
Felix Adler: an ethical culture/ Howard B. Radest.
p. cm.— (American liberal religious thought; vol. 5)
Includes bibliographical references.
1. Adler, Felix, 1851–1933—Ethics. 2. Adler, Felix, 1851–1933—Political and
social views. 3. Ethical culture movement. I. Title. II. Series.
BP605.E84R33   170'.92—dc20   96-42927
ISBN 0-8204-3682-8
ISSN 1080-5389

Die Deutsche Bibliothek-CIP-Einheitsaufnahme

Radest, Howard B.:
Felix Adler: an ethical culture/ Howard B. Radest. –New York; Washington,
D.C./ Baltimore; Boston; Bern; Frankfurt am Main; Berlin; Vienna; Paris: Lang.
(American liberal religious thought; Vol. 5)
ISBN 0-8204-3682-8
NE: GT

© 1998 Peter Lang Publishing, Inc., New York

for
Emma, Jes, Rob and Nora
and for
Brendan, Kara, Mike and Karen

CONTENTS

PREFACE

I confess to a prejudice. I am a Humanist and a member of the Council of Ethical Culture Leaders and have been since 1956. So my interpretation of Felix Adler's thought and work is inevitably shaped by the fact that the movement he founded in 1876 has been and is my spiritual home. After all, the ministry of any faith tends toward apologia rather than discourse. Nevertheless, while I cannot be the judge of my own objectivity, I have tried to avoid doctrinal advocacy and the characteristics of Humanism and Ethical Culture lend themselves to that effort.

It is helpful, in this regard, to recognize the rather atypical relationship of Adler as the "founder" to the movement he founded. This may best be illustrated autobiographically. When I joined Ethical Culture as a leadership-trainee in 1951, I was struck by the fact that nearly all of my future colleagues were likely to be philosophic naturalists rather than Kantian or neo-Kantian idealists. Customarily, our discussions referred to thinkers like John Dewey or Erich Fromm and, in that period, to existentialists like Albert Camus and Jean Paul Sartre as well. Socially and politically, we were liberals and social democrats. Nevertheless, Adler's political ideas, his notion of "organized democracy," of which more later, were scarcely known within the Ethical Society. His economic ideas were ignored and his notion of a "supersensible" realm was mentioned, if at all, with discomfort. In short, while respect and even awe for Adler's practical accomplishments were evident, there was little attention paid to his thought as such and consequently, little appreciation of it as well.

Ironically, Adler himself had encouraged philosophic pluralism at least among the members of his Society if not among his colleagues. As he had said in his inaugural address in May of 1876, Ethical Culture would be committed to "deed before creed," to the responsible and active personal conscience. He sought, in other words, to avoid those conflicts which had led to bloody wars of sect and schism in religion as in politics. By the middle of the 20th Century, however, this pluralism had grown so open-ended that it was difficult to establish legitimate conceptual boundaries once one moved past reference to human worth and dignity and a generalized commitment to a "democratic way of living." Indeed, philosophic niceties were almost dismissed as needless and trivial. In part, no doubt, this was due to the deterioration of philosophy into language games and theology into a rediscovery of sin. But, in no small measure, this pluralism was nurtured within the movement itself by the failure to take Adler's thought seriously enough to attempt a reconstruction. Simultaneously, and despite valiant efforts by leaders like Jerome Nathanson and Horace Friess, no significant alternative was developed.

Typically, most members were committed to practical good works and most leaders addressed themselves to issues of the day, to matters of personal development, and to efforts to distinguish Ethical Culture from other "liberal" religions and, at times, from religion as such. In short, although clearly a movement of the "word," Ethical Culture and Humanism generally exhibited what has been called the "anti-intellectualism" of American life.

No doubt in reaction to the piety of the religious traditions toward their founders, members and leaders alike were emotionally resistant to elevating any single figure to dominance in a movement committed to democracy. Thus, Adler himself called his masterwork, *An Ethical Philosophy of Life.* Symbolically, most of Adler's books were allowed to go out of print. To be sure, those who still recalled Adler personally spoke of him with awe. It was clear enough that he represented a respected and even beloved authority in their lives. And, moreover, the present and future generation of Adler's successors were informed by them in no uncertain terms that they fell far short of the founder's brilliance and abilities.

It was in this setting that I came to work in Ethical Culture. As a trainee I was expected to become familiar with the history and thought of Ethical Culture and so with Adler's work. I confess that, unlike most of my future colleagues, I found his ideas challenging and insightful, although I also confess that his neo-Kantian metaphysics failed to appeal. Trained in Columbia University's philosophy department which was at the time a center of naturalist thought, I was more the pragmatist and naturalist. Nevertheless, Adler struck a chord with me, particularly as he represented the fascinating amalgam of idea and practice which had initially led me toward philosophy. I could reject his cosmology and his Victorianism and still find much that spoke to me and my condition. Moreover, I was convinced, as I learned more and more about his work, that it could speak as well to the modern condition, not just to my own.

In 1968, I had completed my study of the history of Ethical Culture in the United States.[1] So, when in 1970 I came to the task of the doctoral dissertation, it was inevitable that my subject would be Felix Adler. In this I was encouraged by my Columbia teachers who were also leaders in Ethical Culture, Joseph L. Blau and Horace Friess. Other Columbia philosophers like James Gutmann and John Herman Randall Jr. provided a sympathetic and critical resource. And Charles

Frankel, whose Humanism was manifest in his writing as in his teaching, agreed to oversee my efforts. Lawrence Cremin and David Sidorsky as members of the dissertation committee suffered through my less than felicitous efforts. Because of the customary generosity of Professor Friess, I came to examine in some detail two sets of Adler's unpublished lectures that were hardly known at all. In 1894 Adler, at the Plymouth Summer School of Ethics, developed his views of the "labor" question and its consequences for political economy. And, in 1923, while at Oxford to deliver the Hibbert Lectures,[2] Adler also gave four lectures on the implications of culture for education. These lectures shed new light on Adler's views of schooling and of organized democracy and so sent me back to a review of his other published and unpublished work. Out of that effort, the dissertation developed.

The doctorate was completed in 1971. Since that time, I have continued my work with Ethical Culture and, more recently, with the Humanist Institute. I served, too, as Director of the Ethical Culture Fieldston Schools from 1979–1991. Among other things, these experiences led me to explore the relationships of Humanism to the Enlightenment and to Transcendentalism and, in particular, to see how Humanism was an effective response to the irrationalities of post-modernism and of relativism run-wild.[3] Then, in 1995, Creighton Peden and Donald Crosby of the Highlands Institute for American Religious Thought invited me to membership and suggested that my dissertation might be a useful addition to other studies of liberal religion. It was with no little hesitation that I returned to my 1971 effort and to the challenging task of re-writing academic *argot* into what I hope is now readable prose.

As I reviewed my 25 year old thesis in the light of what my future had become since its creation, I was struck by how much of Adler's thought had influenced my own. I echoed to Adler's concerns with "frustration" and its meaning for ethics, with reconstructing democracy, with the interconnections of politics, economics, moral values and personal life. I found, too, that our contemporary discourse on *praxis* was both philosophically and biographically foreshadowed in Adler's work. In short, he remained relevant despite a worn-out metaphysics and an austere Victorianism. In fact, that relevance was one of the surprises that emerged as I pursued my inquiries. And the surprise continues.

I have explored the few items that have appeared since 1971, the work of Robert Guttchen, James F. Hornback, Benny Kraut and, of course, Horace Friess. Where appropriate, I have cited their views in the text and listed their work in the bibliography. Finally, I recognize now, even more than I did 25 years ago, how much I owe to many people. To name them all would be impossible. But, certainly Natalie Koretz, Jean Kotkin, Barbara Michaels and Louis Sapir have demonstrated the continuing depth of commitment to Ethical Culture that Adler hoped for. Above all, my friend, colleague and the former President of the American Ethical Union, Werner Klugman, made this renewed effort possible by the example he offers of all that is worthy and sound in the Ethical Humanism that we share. My family, as usual, has been patient with my efforts which, at times, has meant a bit of neglect and abbreviated visits. And, as has been true for some 45 years now, my wife, Rita, has been there to encourage, criticize and support. Without these many friends and family, and without colleagues whose criticisms have been gentle and to the point, this effort would neither have begun 25 years ago nor been revisited now. As is usual and accurate, they have taught me much. As is equally accurate, any errors and less than felicitous interpretations are my own responsibility.

Notes

[1] Howard B. Radest, _Toward Common Ground_, New York, Ungar, 1969

[2] Felix Adler, _The Reconstruction of The Spiritual Ideal_, New York, D. Appleton and Company, 1923.

[3] Howard B. Radest, _The Devil and Secular Humanism_, New York, Praeger, 1990 and _Humanism With A Human Face_, Westport, Conn. Praeger, 1996.

INTRODUCTION

The Uses of Philosophy

If at all, Felix Adler is discussed and even dismissed, as a neo-Kantian idealist and religious reformer.[1] Certainly these themes shaped his career and marked his contribution to philosophy and religion. But I will explore other interpretations of Adler's place in the history of thought and practice. In doing this I am not denying his Kantianism or his faith. I want, however, to shed light on his contributions in a different way. In turn, this approach will reflect back on his kind of idealism and his kind of reform and perhaps serve further to illuminate them. Thus, I will be looking at Adler on education, on social reform, on politics and on economics. In that way, I can also show that just because he moved between market place, academy and pulpit in a long and busy life, his ideas escape the ordinary boundaries of philosophic and religious categories. Moreover, by extending an exploration of Adler as a man of philosophy and of practice, I believe that we can better appreciate his insights into the moral problems of industrial society and the fact that he foresaw them long before they became part of current discourse.

Adler's work was and is relevant to the modern experience, to our own and to those who came before us. Unfortunately, however, relevance has become a cliché and, during the 1960s, was more likely than not a weapon of politics as theater. Too often, it only means that we have found an ally or an enemy in some struggle or other that we take to be of primary importance. To be "relevant" then identifies someone who agrees with our prejudices, and to be "irrelevant" signifies the sin of refusing to do so. But relevance, no doubt by other names, has a legitimate philosophic and moral status. This arises from the notion that ideas do not live in Plato's "heaven beyond the heavens" but must in some way be responsive to "the problems of men," as John Dewey put it. Relevance points to the pragmatic features of intelligence, to whether or not what we think and say matters at all and to whom. In other words, it is fair to ask any thinker how his or her thought works out, as long as utility is not given a narrow and opportunistic reading.

I would not, however, want to give the impression that Adler's Kantianism can be ignored. His emphasis on rationality and on the constructive activity of reason ought not to be dismissed. Adler's question, however, is how that activity can be brought to bear on

personal development and social problems in the world. As he works
it through, he builds a bridge between the austerity and even flatness
of rationalism and the convulsive complexity of the modern
experience. Adler's problem is not, as it was for Kant, the place of the
human being in a world of determining causal mechanisms. The
"reality producing functions of the human mind" get their content
from Adler's religious, social and political reform and not from
Newtonian physics. Adler's philosophic anthropology portrays an
image of the person as an active and creative agent for the
reconstruction of self and society.[2] To this end, rationality sanctions a
concept of autonomy and speaks to human freedom just as it did for
Kant. But, rationality itself is to be reconstructed. It is a program of
development and not a description of the human soul and its formal
obligations.

It is this pragmatic reading of idealism that John Herman Randall
Jr. describes.

> What is the criterion of a good idealism?...Take science alone and you
> will be missing the most important things in human life, beauty,
> striving, the fight for social justice, God. This is, of course, a "pragmatic
> position" and the Romantic idealists were in one sense all pragmatists.
> The absolute truth we do not and cannot know. "Is it gods or atoms?" The
> important question is, which best guides our actions, which gives us the
> values we want most deeply? Which serves best our living and that of the
> like minded..?[3]

To reconceive Adler's Kantianism along romantic and activist lines,
then, is not an unreasonable proposition.

Philosophically, Adler moved between the *noumenal* and
phenomenal worlds but did not make the sharp dichotomy between
them that was the Kantian habit of an earlier time. The ideal and the
real were connected in action, so Adler's is a participatory
philosophy. It is therefore to the point to explore Adler's realism
about the people he described and the situations in which they found
themselves then, and we still find ourselves, now. To be sure,
philosophy has been tempted by the universal. In fact, however, its
history reflects its particular moment. So, while Adler did at times use
the language of eternity, his project addressed the conditions of
human beings in an industrial and commercial civilization. Looking
at his work today, romantic and existential themes suggest themselves
as well. In any event, system, rationality, coherence are to be the
servants and not the masters.

Of course, any effort to re-interpret and perhaps even to reconstruct a man's thought has its dangers. But Adler's record is a full and accessible one. So it is possible to catch his thought as it developed in word and in act. Over some 60 years, he delivered weekly addresses to the Ethical Society, shared his ideas with the Ethical Culture leaders' seminar, taught his courses at Columbia, and dictated informal notes almost daily to his secretary. Often Adler used these various efforts to test out his ideas with his colleagues. Later he would publish them in more permanent form. Fortunately, it was also possible to talk with men and women whose memories of Adler were still vivid and so to appreciate nuance and response that could not appear on the printed page.[4]

Adler was not a systematic philosopher. Yet, his thinking evolved more or less consistently and certain themes recurred regularly. In his earliest utterances he had addressed the "labor" question, the needs and rights of women and children, education, and religious reform. Above all, he insisted that reform demanded personal action in order to change the way things were done. It was to these themes in experience that he returned over and over again. It is true that, at times, events gave some of them greater emphasis and it is also true that their content became richer as he worked with them, tried them out in practice and learned from those around him. Adler also did not neglect his more technical philosophic inquiries. For example, he continued to worry about the precise status of ethical ideas and the relationship between a *noumenal* world and empirical prescriptions for actual situations.

Adler was finally a philosophic moralist, so it is fair to judge his ideas by their outcomes and by their fruitfulness. As Stephen Toulmin reminds us,

> We might say of the moralist that in him the psychologist, the engineer and the artist meet. The psychologist in him must be knowledgeable about the ways in which people may be expected to feel in different circumstances; the engineer in him must be used to handling the full scale, practical situations of life...and the artist in him must be sensitive enough to recognize those crucial moments when particular rules of conduct must be superseded and to trace out the "features of the soul" in the new stage of its growth. The moralist must study the institutions and practices of society, not simply for what they do but for what they could be made to do...[5]

Adler left a number of practical legacies like the Ethical Culture Fieldston Schools and the Ethical Culture Societies. But, he did not establish a philosophic following. Certainly well known and effective in his own time, it is necessary to assess whether Adler's ideas can live in the present. Failing that he, like so many others, becomes only a vanished and interesting moment in the history of ideas and social reform.

Idealism and Reality

As I reviewed the record in order to interpret Adler's thought, a number of likely organizing themes suggested themselves as useful for my analysis. Their connection is to be found in the idea of culture, which was for Adler a self-conscious process of personal and social development. Nurture, growth, and development would capture his intention. Dynamically viewed, culture is education, and education properly understood is culture. For Adler, then, education was not concerned only with schooling, with the relationships of teacher and student, with problems of method and content, with the psychology of learning. Each of these, to be sure, played a role for him as he established and built the Ethical Culture Schools for which he served as Rector for some 60 years until his death in 1933. But education was essentially a way of both developing an ideal politics, economics and religion and of judging the actual practices to be found in those institutions that in fact existed. The educational *motif*, moreover, identifies the point of it all: that social institutions are instruments for helping human beings to shape themselves morally and, in the process, to participate in shaping others morally as well. Then, too, education connotes development toward an ideal end which, for Adler, was a deliberate and deliberative activity. Thus, reconstruction begins to acquire its content.

As Adler put it, the "ethical act is the most individual act." Ethics is not, therefore, conformity to some universal law. Typically, he re-stated the "categorical imperative" as: "so act as to elicit the best in others and thereby in oneself." Kant's "kingdom of ends" became Adler's spiritual democracy. Already, as we can see, he is moving away from a Kantian legalism.

Before proceeding to empirical themes like labor, politics and economics, I need to describe the way that Adler situated ethics in the idea of the worth and the uniqueness of the person, and this I attempt in Chapter 2. The experience that stirs this concern for Adler is the problem of identity and alienation in industrial society.[6] Ethical individuation is his response. But Adler had criticized Kant's ethics as "too individualistic" and American society for its uncaring *laissez faire* individualism. So, Adler gives a social turn to individuation by holding that in order to become uniquely oneself, one needs reciprocal interaction with others who, in turn, are becoming uniquely themselves. His individualism, then, is at the same time a theory of mutuality, of society. As he put it, "to ethicize and to organize are the same thing." "To organize" has a biological reference and builds on the imagery of organism which, for Adler, replaced the mechanism of his eighteenth century philosophic heritage.

Continuing his response to industrial society, Adler develops his theory of vocation as a practical and as an ideal answer to the "labor" question. As it were, he reconstructs the religious notion of the "calling" in a secular and modern idiom. Thus, the cultured person is the working person, and all persons can become cultured. But work is not the drudgery of factory labor or the specialism of the expert. Indeed, these are the moral problems of industrial labor and the motivation for critical revision. Typically, Adler also finds in the fact of the universalization of labor the opportunity for its reform. The theme is personal productivity which is natural and essential to human nature. By contrast, a consumerist society and its mass-produced goods only reveal the deterioration of personality and so the absence of morally legitimate productivity. In schooling, therefore, he tries to bring together the requirements of technology and commerce and what we would call the liberal arts. He is simultaneously a classicist and a modernist. Setting himself against class concepts, he addresses democratic reconstruction as well by using vocation as a way of reorganizing political representation and election. By identifying work with culture, he challenges the notion that culture is an aristocratic privilege, a gentleman's accoutrement or a mere leisure-time hobby. A radical isolation of work and play makes no moral sense. For the development of these ideas, see Chapter 3.

Religion too must be reconstructed, and not simply because human knowledge has subverted traditional cosmologies and anthropologies. Adler certainly kept up with the debates about Darwinism, and he was expert in religious scholarship. The "higher criticism" of the Bible, the comparative study of religions and mythologies and the results of archeological and anthropological research were very much a part of his continuing study and teaching. His library, for example, included just about every current publication in these fields and in a number of languages. He was a voracious reader. But, more importantly, religious reconstruction was required on ideal and moral grounds as well. The problem was not merely academic. Again beginning with a traditional notion, the soul, Adler moves towards a philosophy of character development. But this is not simply an empirical and psychological project. At the most intimate levels of being, awareness emerges in interaction with other emerging selves. Adler's self is a social self, although it retains a certain privacy as well. The soul, then, is the subject of Chapter 4.

Finally, in order to recapture the Aristotelian connection between ethics and politics, Adler attempts yet another reconstruction. The comfortable and cozy city-state and the openness of an agricultural society are not available in industrial society. So the locus and legitimacy of power must be re-examined in the light of the new size of things. The key, for Adler, is the notion of competence which he identifies with vocation and which thus provides a functional bridge between ethics, economics and politics. The power of judging, deciding and acting arises from the specialty, the unique ability and potency in the possession of the unique human being. The problem then becomes the design of a social order in which the members of the various specialties can have their voice and still be related to each other across specialty lines. As we see in Chapter 5, vocation is an ethical response to the political as well as to the labor question.

Taken together, education, culture and vocation speak to the person as such. Yet, each of these has its social corollary. It is possible, in other words, to reformulate them as proposals for the reform of society and not just for the development of the person's moral character. So, for example, an ethical society would be one in which the uniqueness of each person was recognized, nurtured and protected by all other persons. A truly religious society would evolve around the mutuality and individuality of its communicants. It would be neither monarchical nor hierarchical and, as evolving, would not be imprisoned by outdated metaphysical notions.

Each of Adler's themes is a deliberate challenge to tradition, and each has its import for schooling. Thus vocation speaks to the reconstruction of the school, to the nature of teacher training and to the structure and content of the curriculum. In this context, Adler's own experiments with building and running a school put him among the earliest progressives, although he rejected the term no doubt because of its naturalist and instrumentalist associations. There is throughout all of Adler's discussions of these themes a democratic and an industrial reference as well. Thus, his reconstructions are built around the need to individualize personality in a world of goods, services, money and work.

A final way of stating Adler's project is to re-state his themes as cultural propositions. Culture is the process of self and social consciousness and so appears empirically under the sub-themes of psychology and history. As such, it touches all human experience, turning it into an activity, a participation, and not merely a receptivity. Seen religiously, it is the discovery, emergence and interaction of self with self when at their most exposed and intimate. The soul is thus pluralized, socialized and democratized. Politically, culture leads toward the use of power and vocational competence in order to move to a just social order which Adler called "organized democracy." In economics, culture is the transformation of labor from drudgery to productivity. And each of these is, in its own way, to be an education which is not, therefore, only one institution among many. Instead, it is the obligation of religion, politics and economics to be educational. Ultimately, education is intended for the moral ideal and so, reciprocally, is a politics as well.[7] In a sense, and quite reminiscent of Dewey's use of adverbial language,[8] Adler's thought is an exploration of processes and not of objects and their properties. He is in his own way a philosopher of experience, a genuine modernist.

From Reform To Reconstruction

Felix Adler was born in Alzey, Germany in 1851. Arriving in New York in 1857 after a stormy seventeen day crossing with his father Samuel, his mother, Henrietta and his older brother, Isaac, age eight, the family moved into a pleasant neighborhood near Stuyvesant Square in New York City. Samuel, nearly fifty years old, was to be the Rabbi of Temple Emanuel, then as now one of the leading Jewish Reform congregations in the country. Nearby was the Academy of Music. A bit south was the Cooper Union with its library, lectures and concerts.

The city with its confusions and its promises was to be the setting for Felix Adler's long and productive life. The New York in which he grew up and the America of the second half of the 19th Century were scenes of energies, achievements and disasters. Young Adler's boyhood experience was punctuated by the Civil War and the question of the Union. In the Adler home, Lincoln was an idol and an ideal, and anti-slavery a cause. Symptomatically, as Adler recalled, on the morning after Lincoln's assassination, "I was then fourteen years of age. I came down to the breakfast table and found my father weeping. I had never seen tears in his eyes before."[9]

In the post-war-era that was Adler's teen-age setting, Reconstruction soon gave way to business as usual. Jim Crow and the KKK soon made peonage a way of life for many of the "emancipated." Corruption in public life and unchecked ambition in private life seemed to be turning democracy into a moral tragedy and farce all at once. Commercialism was the boast of American destiny, and the country's heroes were the apostles of industrial greed. Also woven into the tapestry of Adler's biography were the developing social and biological sciences. Reason and knowledge seemed to know no boundaries. Liberation, like corruption, played its role in Adler's development.

But Felix Adler's life cannot be understood only as a response to the big events in the world. The family and the congregational life played their important roles in his development too. Samuel Adler was a creature of the Enlightenment. He had been active while in Germany in both secular struggles for freedom and in Jewish religious reform. The father thus exemplified the marriage of a passion for justice, and for scholarship and this combination was to be crucial in shaping the young and the mature Felix Adler.

The family home was filled with books. Indeed, one of the largest and best collections of *Judaica* in New York City was to be found there. The family's friends and visitors, many of them congregants of the Temple, were men and women of recognized achievement in the life of the city and of the nation. Mostly German Jews, they were the successful immigrants who had made their way in business, finance and the professions. They were thus visible symbols of the American dream. By way of example, the names that appear in Felix Adler's later life include the Seligmans, the Sutros, the Prices, the Morgenthaus, the Bambergers. Music, art and literature played their role in the family's ambiance too.

Samuel inevitably sought the best in education for his sons. After a brief trial of the local public schools, he enrolled them in the Columbia Grammar School, which despite the similarity of name had no affiliation with the University that was later to be Adler's intellectual home. At Columbia Grammar young Felix got a rigorous classical education in Greek and Latin, in modern languages, literature and mathematics. Although intellectually stimulating, Felix's adolescent years were not the happiest. One of the very few Jews in the school and the only one in his class, he recalled, "A Jewish boy from a family largely German among typically American boys of the wealthy class, I found I was forced back upon myself by lack of companionship."[10] He was, according to the family, a "dreamy" boy without the "tough" mindedness of his father or older brother.

Fortunately, Adler's education was not confined to the classroom. With his mother, he shared the charitable rounds characteristic of the life of the Jewish community. Accompanying her, he visited the sick, the poor and the aged. As a teen-ager, he taught in the Temple's Sunday School and was recognized as an effective and popular teacher. Even in these early years, Adler was showing those features of personality which were to be sharpened and matured as he grew older. He developed a love of languages. Consequently, his scholarship was to become formidable, and he found himself at home in classical languages and in modern literatures as well. Encouraged by his father, at age eighteen he regularly delivered sermons at the Hebrew Orphan Asylum, revealing his power with the spoken word and the pulpit style.

On graduation from Columbia Grammar, Felix entered Columbia College. We know very little of his undergraduate years except that he expressed disappointment at the College's lack of broad philosophic interest and intellectual magnanimity. Columbia then no doubt still reflected the Christian parochialism of its origins, which suited neither Adler's temperament nor his interests. Following graduation in 1870, Adler went abroad for graduate study. He first enrolled at the University of Berlin where he began to develop a serious interest in philosophy. This, by the way, troubled his family, particularly his older brother because, to him, philosophy lacked concreteness and practicality. He also studied for the rabbinate at Abraham Geiger's seminary, although he did not complete his studies there. But the Berlin arrangements did not work out, and he transferred to Heidelberg. There, in 1873, he completed his degree in Semitic studies.

Once again, Adler's intellectual needs were met, but his personal life was less than happy. A fellow student recalled, "I...know that he was unmercifully twitted by the students who called him, der Amerikanische Adler (the American eagle)."[11] Later, in his autobiographical notes, Adler expressed his dismay at his fellow students' immoral behavior.[12] Nevertheless, Adler did discover that philosophic climate which his undergraduate education had lacked. He spoke warmly of his studies with Hermann Cohen and of his first exposure to socialism. Although he rejected the Kantianism that Cohen taught and the socialism then popular, he was to be shaped by both. Significantly, it was Friedrich Albert Lange's *Die Arbeiterfrage* which as he said, "opened for me a wide and tragic prospect." A life-long interest in the labor movement and in the problems of industrial society was already beginning to appear.

Two Kantian notions about religion and ethics came to play a significant role in Adler's philosophic development. Kant had shown, at least to Adler's satisfaction, that the existence or non-existence of God could not be demonstrated by "pure reason." Contradictory conclusions could be drawn from the same data. More affirmatively, "practical reason," morality, could be developed without reliance on theology. The "autonomy" and "centrality" of ethics thus became guiding philosophic ideas for Adler and were the critical basis of his reconstruction of religion through the Ethical Culture Societies.

Adler's Jewish and European experiences do not tell the entire story of his development. Nineteenth century American intellectual and religious life cannot be understood without attending to the role of Ralph Waldo Emerson. It is revealing, by way of example, that Adler's earliest colleagues in Ethical Culture, Stanton Coit, William M. Salter, S. Burns Weston and Walter Sheldon, each referred to Emerson in their spiritual biographies.[13] Adler himself singled out Emerson, along with Jesus and the Hebrew Religion, as "formative influences." While much later he denied the lasting importance of Emerson to his philosophy, Adler remained far more Emersonian than he knew or admitted. The search for a "free religion," for a purely "ethical religion" and the insistence on "self reliance" played a part in Adler's thought throughout his life. His emphasis on the unique personality in an organic social relationship with all other unique personalities sings the Emersonian song of the "over soul." And it is surely reasonable to hear Emerson's ode to talent in Adler's vocationalism.

On Adler's return to America, it was assumed that he would eventually succeed his father at the Temple.[14] But it was not to be. On the Sabbath, October 11, 1873, Adler delivered his first and last sermon there, although that was not his intention. His topic was "The Judaism of the Future." Although much of the sermon was characteristic of Jewish reform and modernist scholarship, his message was unmistakably secular, universalist and activist. Thus,

> The question for us to answer now is not...this reform or that reform...(but) is religion about to perish...?
> ...religion not confined to church or synagogue alone shall go forth into the market place...laying its greatest stress not on the believing but in the acting out. A religion such as Judaism ever claimed to be, *not of the creed but of the deed*.....
> ...we discard the narrow spirit of exclusion and loudly proclaim that *Judaism was not given to the Jews alone* but that its destiny is to embrace in one great moral state the whole family of men....[15]

Much later, Adler was to recall the occasion in an interview. "...Some members brought up the fact that I had not mentioned God....The committee came to me and asked whether I believed in God. I said, 'yes, but not in your God....'"[16] The family's historic calling was now closed to him. He was obviously unprepared for business life, although "there was a story in the family that they thought he wouldn't amount to much in a professional way and that maybe they had better look around for some place for him in the jewelry business."[17]   And academic appointments for Jews were hardly to be found.   Fortunately, however, through the good offices and financial support of several leading members of the congregation, Felix was appointed non-resident Professor of Hebrew and Oriental Literature at Cornell University.

From 1873 through 1875 Adler served Cornell as a brilliant and successful teacher.   In his courses he traced a direct line between Pharisaic Judaism and the American ideal.   Scholarship was already morally instrumental in his thinking.   As the only Jew on the faculty, Adler was attacked in the denominational press, accused of atheism and of being a threat to the Christian faith of the students.   While Andrew D. White, the university president, defended Adler, his appointment was not renewed.   The question of vocation was unresolved.   However, some of those who had heard the Temple Sermon invited Adler to speak on the "plan of a new organization." In his address on May 15, 1876 at Standard Hall in New York City he concluded, "Diversity in the creed, unanimity in the deed....This is the common ground where we may all grasp hands...united in mankind's common cause."[18]

With that lecture, Ethical Culture was born, and it rapidly built a record of achievement.   During its first decade it established a free kindergarten which evolved into the Ethical Culture Fieldston Schools, a district nursing service which grew into the Visiting Nurse Service , a tenement building company, the University Settlement and a bit later projects that were to become the Legal Aid Society and the Child Study Association.   Classes in the moral education of children were offered and new Ethical Culture Societies were established in Philadelphia, Chicago and St. Louis.

Clearly, Adler exhibited formidable powers and apparently inexhaustible energies.   Practical demands, however, overrode any possibility of doing serious philosophy and the rather simple notion of an "ethical" religion as such seemed sufficient at the time.   Adler was a brilliant and challenging public speaker.   As one observer wrote, "His sentences seem to drop out of a great profound."   Adler was also attracting attention.   Another observer reported, "Two hundred new members have joined the New York Society for Ethical Culture in the past year (1878-79) nearly doubling its membership.   Standard Hall no longer accommodates the audiences and next season the Society will occupy Chickering Hall...."[19]

While living a public and demanding life, Adler also managed to fall in love and start a family. In 1880 he married Helen Goldmark, the daughter of a successful Brooklyn chemist and businessman. Patterns of family life based on his own childhood years were begun early for the new family and persisted. For example, during the summers the family, which eventually came to include two sons and three daughters, spent its time at Keene Valley in the Adirondacks. There, Adler would devote his mornings to study and writing. For the rest, there were games and walks and the visits of friends and colleagues. At meal-times, very much the *pater familias*, he would formally share the things he was thinking about with the family and their guests.

Adler was also part of an evolving liberal religious neighborhood. Thus, in 1878, he was elected president of the Free Religious Association, which had been founded in 1866 by Francis Ellingwood Abbott and O.B. Frothingham. It counted among its members Emerson, Lucretia Mott, Wendell Phillips and Julia Ward Howe. Repeatedly Adler tried to move the Association toward action. But for a group of individualists, resistance to organization was endemic, and besides they feared it might lead to a new clericalism. Finally, in 1882, Adler resigned in protest. As Stowe Persons writes, "...Adler's patience was exhausted...Although he remained heartily in favor of the principles of the Free Religious Platform, he was disgusted with the scrupulousness of the Association's policy..."[20] With that, it is fair to conclude that the focus of Adler's vocation narrowed to his work with the Ethical Culture Societies.

In the first decade since the May 15th address Adler was working out the lines of his future development. By his fortieth year he was a successful and acknowledged member of the community of social, educational and religious reformers. As he moved into the 1890s, however, he began more and more to address the philosophic import of his practical and institutional efforts. Thus, in 1891, Adler spent a sabbatical year in Europe and, no doubt, reflected on the dangers of losing himself in what he came to call "this reform or that reform..." The "deed" remained at the center, to be sure, but the "creed" could not be ignored.

Symbolic of this subtle shift of attention, "deed not creed" became "deed before creed." Also revealing was the fact that Adler founded the *International Journal of Ethics* in 1890, which is still published today as *Ethics* by the University of Chicago. In its pages were to be found the essays of American philosophers, idealists and religious scholars, naturalists like William James, John Dewey and G. H. Mead, as well as those of British idealists and utilitarians. For a time, at least, it almost seemed that Adler's move would be onto a global, or at least Western, stage. Ethical Culture Societies existed in many western European countries, Great Britain and Japan. By 1896, an International Ethical Union had been established. Adler became a regular visitor to the Continent.

In 1902, Adler was named Professor of Political and Social Ethics at Columbia University and continued to teach there until his death, while also serving as leader of the Ethical Society. In 1908, he was appointed Theodore Roosevelt Professor at the University of Berlin. Through the International Ethical Union, Adler developed the International Moral Education Congresses, which began in 1908. In 1911, working with Gustav Spiller of the international movement, he helped to organize the first International Races Congress. Later, in 1923, he was asked to give the Hibbert Lectures at Oxford. Adler thus moved comfortably between the Ethical Society, the academy, the city and the international world. Yet, while he found his international colleagues stimulating, they were much "too academic." The decades between 1890 and 1920 confirmed his view that the moral reconstruction of industrial society could best be understood and attempted from an American base. Adler was clearly an advocate of American exceptionalism. America, for all its faults, was still the "city on a hill."

During that same time, the United States was experiencing its own move onto the world stage, and Adler, characteristically, responded. For example, he was in the forefront of those who criticized American imperialism in Latin America and the Philippines. From 1898 onward, he began to raise the issue of what he came to call the "national crisis." With World War I and Woodrow Wilson's League of Nations, Adler believed the crisis had reached a climactic moment. The war was not a democratic crusade but only an arena of conflicting imperialisms, the League an alliance of the victors. At home, the tension between "manifest destiny" and spiritual democracy was growing. So, if the American model was to be an ethical model, this tension had to be exposed and the illusions of American self-righteousness dispelled. The nation itself had to be "ethicized."

A deep and pervasive attention to what we call "minority rights" appeared at the center of Adler's thought. The "labor" question had been an original interest and child labor particularly troubling. The civil war and the Lincoln influence had put racial justice on Adler's agenda. But now, Adler saw these issues as another part of the "national crisis" and as a world problem as well. In spite of the criticism of many of his colleagues in the Ethical Societies, he opposed the popular movement for woman's suffrage but on the grounds that the "vote" merely made a superficial adjustment to a flawed institution. It was an example of merely "quantitative democracy." At the same time, Adler believed it necessary to open careers and professions to women and to understand that motherhood too was a vocation. In short, Adler didn't seem to fit into the convenient compartments labeled radical or conservative.

As the nineteenth century ended and the first decades of the twentieth century passed, Adler was convinced that whatever the details of this issue or that, civilization itself was in deep moral trouble. The struggle for the rights of labor continued to meet with violent and bloody repression. Private armies, strikes, unemployment and economic depression were joined with the absence of a political will to respond justly. World War was only a continuation of industrial history. It was in 1891 that, prophetically, Adler together with Crawford Howell Toy of Harvard and Henry Carter Adams of Michigan had founded the Summer School of Applied Ethics to address the coming crisis. Among its teachers were William James, Josiah Royce and Jane Addams. It was there in 1894 that Adler delivered twelve lectures on the ethical problems of a commercial and industrial society, opening up his new theme of "organized democracy."

In the next years and until his death in 1933, the theme was expanded. Three major books appeared that had grown out of his lectures, his addresses at the Ethical Society, his Columbia courses and the Ethical Culture leaders seminar. The first, more topical but still embedded in his philosophic ideas, was *The World Crisis and Its Meaning* (1916). The second was *An Ethical Philosophy Of Life* (1918) which summed up the practical and philosophic conclusions of a life-time. And finally, *The Reconstruction of the Spiritual Ideal* (1924) carried these ideas forward as a criticism of the "false" civilization that had been exposed by World War I.

As Adler evolved his philosophy of industrial society, his thoughts inevitably turned back to education and schooling. So, already in his seventies and nearing the end of his life, he became more and more explicit about the connection between social and pedagogical radicalism. He began to dream of a major new step in education. As he said to his Board of Trustees,

> we should...give rein to our vastest hopes...think of the future graduates
> of the business school as playing a great role in the world....The white
> races are one third of the population of the world; the colored races...are
> showing their restiveness under the domination of the white...the
> commercial spirit is everywhere breaking the hearts of the races....The

greatest change that the world needs today is the creation of real men....We must dedicate our pre-vocational school...to the future civilization of this planet.[21]

In the 1890s a concept of "organic" education was emerging. The School was no longer to be just another example of "good works," no longer just the Workingman's School. The student body was diversified. The curriculum integrated classical studies, modern science, industrial arts and ethics. Dramatic performance and studio arts were not treated as "frills" or as "co-curricular" but as essentials. In 1913, an experimental Arts High School had been established. Then, in 1926, Adler announced the "prevocational school of business" and the "ideals for the new school:"

we go through the whole history of commerce...the kind of government it has promoted; how it has influenced science and the arts...how far commerce was the accomplice of tyranny; how far commerce today is a menace in the Far East...We give the young business men...an idea...of the policies to be favored in national and international life, of the attitude to be taken toward fellow workers...we endeavor to implant in them the principle of watching their lives and estimating their own value by the way in which they affect other people, to bring that principle into the very market place.[22]

The Fieldston Plan, as it came to be called, was to be the last major act in his life. With it, the mature Adler still reflected the energies of the younger man as critic and educator and now as philosopher. The *ad hoc* radicalism of the pulpit had become an organized radicalism. And to the last, Adler remained a man of the academy and the market place. Tutored by a community that was economically and socially privileged, he ended as a radical democrat moving from *noblesse oblige* to spiritual democracy. The eighty-two years of Adler's life were marked by transitional struggles here and around the globe to which he had inevitably and characteristically responded. Although he never deserted the call of the moral ideal, he remained to the end a realist. And while the real had to be "ethicized," it could not be ignored. So he avoided the illusions of utopianism and the trap of opportunism.

As with anyone whose career is in the public arena, there is, finally, the danger of taking the image and role for the man. Yet, as Julius Henry Cohen remarked, Adler "was fuller of real fun, prankish, impish fun than any man I have met." But the role dominated the record so we rarely get a glimpse of the intimate Adler. A letter to Helen Adler from Europe, however, reveals it.

> It is all so tantalizingly beautiful and so tantalizingly unsatisfactory. We must hope and plan and arrange somehow that we shall take this lovely trip together...But in the meantime, my own particular lady love, there cannot possibly be a closer response than that of my thoughts to yours as they travel over the leagues of sea, annihilating space and defying separation. This makes me happy despite all grumbling and so I will sign for tonight your discontented, yet deeply contented,
>
> Felix[23]

His chapters on failure and frustration, particularly in his final three books are not just abstract considerations but personal confessions. And occasionally, even his formal addresses open up an insight into character:

> has not your experience told you, I think mine has, that those who put on the hardness of inflexible rigor are often persons who realize that they are subject to deep emotions and who fear to be carried by their softer feelings...and who thus assume a sternness which is not really natural to them?[24]

As the members of the Ethical Societies, the students, teachers, business people, social workers and artists he came in touch with tell us, he helped people literally to change their lives. And yet, despite his accomplishments, he lived with a sense of inadequacy mingled with a persistent long-range optimism. As he said to his Board of Trustees in 1929, "I think that the lamp which we lit in the darkness of the storm may in future centuries be... plunged into darkness and be again rekindled..."[25]

Although failing physically in his last years, Adler's mind remained clear. He spoke occasionally from the Ethical Platform, met with his students and continued to raise funds for the school. He attended the Ethical Culture leaders' seminar until the Fall of 1932. Algernon Black recalled that last appearance,

> He had on his frock coat....It was late afternoon in autumn...the golden sunlight from the west came into the room and shone on the beautiful rug and on him. He started to read....He got about two sentences into his paper and he got lost....He started over again...and got lost again. Very slowly and deliberately, he took out his watch...a gold watch, and he

pressed a little button and opened it. Then he said, "I guess my time is up." Slowly, he closed it and walked out....[26]

Still, ten days before his death, he was discussing a foundation grant for the Fieldston School with V.T. Thayer, the School's Director. Finally, on April 24, 1933, Felix Adler died after a long struggle with cancer.

Notes

[1] For example, see, Joseph L. Blau, *Men and Movements in American Philosophy*, New York, Prentice Hall, 1952, pp.193-194; John Herman Randall, Jr., "The Churches and the Liberal Tradition," *The Annals of the American Academy of Political and Social Science*, March 1948, pp.148-164; Herbert W. Schneider, *A History of American Philosophy*, New York, Columbia University Press, 1946, pp.462-464. Horace Friess, Adler's son-in-law and literary executor, maintained that ultimately Adler's ideas would be a lasting contribution to the development of religious thought (see *Felix Adler and Ethical Culture*, edited by Fannia Weingartner, New York, Columbia University Press, 1981, Chapter 17).

[2] The term, "reconstruction" is typical of both Adler and John Dewey and suggests their philosophic kinship, despite the fact that Adler was an idealist and Dewey an instrumentalist and empiricist.

[3] *The Career of Philosophy*, Volume 2, New York, Columbia University Press, 1965, p.204.

[4] Among other resources, I had the benefit of some 50 or more oral histories that were completed during the 1960's as part of the project to develop the story of the Ethical Societies in the United States. In addition, Horace Friess reviewed these pages when they were first written and shared his critical comments with me.

[5] *Reason in Ethics*, London, Cambridge University Press, 1960, p.178.

[6] Adler, of course, was familiar with Hegel's views on alienation, although he did not allude to them specifically (see, G.W.F. Hegel, *The Phenomenology of Mind*, translated by J. B. Baillie, New York, Harper and Row, 1967). He was surely familiar with socialist ideas on labor, productivity and alienation in capitalist societies, although he probably did not know Karl Marx's *Economic and Philosophical Manuscripts* of 1844. For the latter, see Erich Fromm, *Marx's Concept of Man*, New York, Ungar, 1966, in which these manuscripts are translated by T. B. Bottomore.

[7] For a general discussion of the notion of schooling as a politics, see "Schooling And The Search For A Usable Politics," Howard B. Radest, in *History, Religion and Spiritual Democracy*, edited by Maurice

Wohlgelernter, New York, Columbia University Press, 1980, Chapter 15.

[8] See the use of the term "religious" in John Dewey, *A Common Faith*, New Haven, Yale University Press, 1934.

[9] Horace L. Friess, *Felix Adler and Ethical Culture*, edited by Fannia Weingartner, New York, Columbia University Press, 1981, p.21.

[10] Friess, *Adler*, p.20.

[11] From a letter to Gideon Chagy by Dr. Adolphe de Castro, December 17, 1948, Ethical Culture Archive, New York City.

[12] *An Ethical Philosophy of Life*, New York, D. Appleton-Century, 1918, pp.11-13.

[13] For a discussion of this group and their relationship to Adler, see James F. Hornback, *The Philosophic Sources and Sanctions of the Founders of Ethical Culture*, unpublished doctoral dissertation, New York, Columbia University, 1983.

[14] For an effective discussion of Felix Adler's relationship to Judaism, see Benny Kraut, *The Religious Evolution of Felix Adler*, Cincinnati, Hebrew Union College Press, 1979.

[15] "The Temple Emanuel Sermon," Archive.

[16] "Obituary, Felix Adler," *The New York Times*, April 25, 1933.

[17] From a conversation with Horace Friess.

[18] "Inaugural Address," Archive.

[19] Regular reports on Adler and the Ethical Culture Societies are to be found in *The Index*, The Journal of the Free Religious Association, 1877, 1878.

[20] *Free Religion*, New Haven, Yale University Press, 1947, p.96.

[21] *Minutes*, Board of Trustees, The New York Society for Ethical Culture, November 1925.

[22] *Ideals For Our New School*, pamphlet, February 1926, no page numbers.

[23] August 20, 1896, Archive

[24] "In Commemoration of the Centennial Anniversary of the Death of Immanuel Kant," January 24, 1904, Archive, p.18.

[25] *Minutes*, Board of Trustees, New York Society for Ethical Culture, October 1929.

[26] From an interview with Algernon D. Black, 1963.

II

CULTURE AND THE ETHICAL IDEAL

Ethical Experience

Every ideal is intended to be a relief from some sort of spiritual pain.
Ideals are pain born; they are the offspring of suffering...The history of
religions might be written in terms of the particular types of inner pain
which respectively they were designed to alleviate...[1]

Written by Adler in 1923, these words are a poignant reminder of
the trauma that the War had inflicted on the reformer and his or her
condition in the postwar world. The liberal children of the
Enlightenment were living through what they felt was the betrayal of
their ideals and dreams. The hopefulness of a scientific, democratic
and industrial culture, and the inevitability of progress, seemed but an
illusion. As the liberals saw it, the parties to the war, the "civilized"
nations of Europe, had behaved as vicious and violent barbarians.
The nations that had given us Shakespeare, Rousseau, Da Vinci and
Goethe, that had invented parliamentary democracy and nurtured
modern science, were no more morally advanced than their allegedly
less enlightened ancestors and neighbors. The peace conference had
revealed them all as greedy, selfseeking and shortsighted. With the
War that did not "make the world safe for democracy" and the peace
that was no peace, the 18th Century dream of a perfectible world, the
belief in the benevolent nature of things social and personal, was
suddenly and radically in doubt. In response a bit later, religion,
deserting the Social Gospel, was to discover sin again in the
ministrations of neoorthodoxy. The failure of civilization
transcended the ordinary failures and frustrations of biography and
locality.
For Adler, however, the war and the peace were only another
moment in history that confirmed his view that the crisis was to be
found in industrial society itself. As he put it on America's entry into
the war,

It is a trifle trying to one's patience to hear these weak meowings that
civilization has broken down. No, civilization has not broken down.
The war has demonstrated that what we believed was civilization was not
civilization...we should now get together to try to build up a real

civilization instead of trying to build up a money civilization and a power
civilization...[2]

To be sure, as a counselor and Ethical Culture leader Adler had
met with suffering, illness and death often enough. As a reformer, he
had seen projects fail or as likely, take unforeseen and undesired
turns. But, typically, he had interpreted these not just as existential
facts of personal life but as instances of a wide and even metaphysical
gulf between what "is" and what "ought" to be. The finite world
could never ultimately be "ethicized." At the same time, the effort to
do so was a condition of human development. Thus, Adler, unlike his
Enlightenment colleagues, lived with a tragic sense of moral
experience. The metaphysical gulf was a permanent fact of human
life, both a stimulus to action and a guarantee of failure.

Ever the moralist, Adler gave tragedy a personal as well as a
social dimension. And so, in the postwar world, he again returned to
the theme of frustration now felt even more acutely as he was aware
that he was nearing the end of his life with his own life project
inevitably incomplete. It is against this background that he wrote of
the sources of "spiritual pain,"

> First, the sense of the insignificance of man in this wide
> universe...never has the Lilliputian disparity between man and the
> magnitude of his world, the immensities of space come home with such
> crushing force as it has to our own generation...
>
> The second note of pain which is felt far more acutely at present
> than at any other time, is due to the fate of those innumerable fellow
> beings who perish by the wayside while mankind slowly and awkwardly
> tries to achieve progress...
>
> The third problem is constituted by the need of relief from the
> intolerable strain of the divided conscience...the divided conscience...is
> felt by men who are eagerly desirous to make their life whole...and who do
> not see how to do it because they find that the ethical standard...in their
> private relations...is incapable...to guide them where they are required to
> act as members of groups...[3]

Felt inwardly by "ethically sensitive minds," spiritual pain is also
a sign of moral presence. Free and rational beings feel it, but things
cannot. Culturally, it gets its content from the "historical situation"
which is, however, not its cause but its "evocative occasion." In form,
then, spiritual pain is ever-present in human experience. Neither
messianic nor utopian, Adler insists that our lives will always be

burdened by moral inadequacies. That is the human condition to which any moment in history brings its particular substance.

With this in mind, Adler turns from the perennial situation to the historic moment. Industrial society gives more than sufficient evidence of misery and the divided conscience. Disintegrated living is its style, and alienation its outcome. Already evident in the factories of the 19th century, the early 20th Century further perfected the division of labor with the development of "scientific management" and industrial "rationalization." These techniques of what was called "human engineering" insured even more of the fragmentation and specialism that Adler had begun to criticize in his earliest years. For the sake of productivity, the worker at work was to be treated as an object or an instrument and not as a person.[4] Aristocracies and moneyed elites accrued more and more power even as a democratic rhetoric grew louder and louder. Parenthetically, as we know, the gap between rich and poor has hardly closed and indeed assumes worldwide dimension. To be sure, there are plenty of goodies to be distributed, but the underlying moral problem is not touched. Nor has our rhetoric grown quieter and less self-righteous in our own time. Adler, then, was prophetic as well as critical.

As Adler saw it, ethics was retreating from the public life into the academy. Religion, caught in the trap of dated theologies, was helpless. Science, boasting moral neutrality in the name of objectivity, simply refused to deal with the industrial problem. Meanwhile, men and women were coming to live in new kinds of groups but without the ethical and political resources necessary for building decent relationships between labor and management, nation and nation. Adler, then, was forced to a double attack on Christian and on Kantian ethics. Having focused almost exclusively on individual salvation and conduct, both have neglected the social dimensions of experience. On the other side as it were, social scientists, social reformers and socialists were preoccupied with issues of collectivity to the neglect of persons. Against these tendencies, Adler looks for a "third" way.

The issue for the individual is how to regard himself or herself and how to be treated by others as an "end *per se.*"[5] For society, the problem is mutuality and inclusiveness, *i.e.*, the relationships of persons to each other as unique and as equal beings but also as creatures of traditions and histories. Of course, there will always be tensions between person and person and between persons and society, but this need not necessarily lead to the kind of conflict that ends with winners and losers. The self is still a social self; society is still an outcome of personal moral agency. In short, Adler's question becomes more and more urgent: how is an ethical life to be possible in an industrial society? The reply needs both a practical and a philosophic dimension else we are left with momentary reforms and empty ideas.

The Idea of Worth

Adler had neither the benefit nor the handicap of revelation. Convinced that America was still the moral frontier, he was in a position to think beyond tradition. This had been the burden of Emerson's message in essays like "The Divinity School Address" and "The American Scholar." It continued to ring true for Adler. So, as he set out to develop his moral base line, he admitted that he was dealing with "attributions," "assumptions" and "postulates." He was, in other words, working out an axiology. On the other hand, ever the realist, he knew that ethics was not mathematics and that not just any set of coherent axioms would do. He therefore coupled his postulational effort with his notion of "ethical experience." Human beings felt obligations, knew they had duties, made choices and assessed consequences and in all of these distinguished between better and worse, good and bad. They were, as we would put it today, "ethical animals." In fact, whenever matters of human relationships became problematic and whenever the problematic was confessed, ethical experience was present. But as experience, it could neither demonstrate nor refute moral principle. It was exhibitory and pedagogical. The moral ground then had to be secured on other and nonempirical ground. So Adler was still in his own way the Kantian of whom he said, "for he has taught men not so much philosophy as to philosophize...."[6] While he never addressed it systematically, his method consisted in moving back and forth between event and meaning.

Yet another essential feature of his approach to the problem of ethics was the imperative of personal activity. The moral agent was a participant in and not an observer of events. Adler was quite explicit about all of this.

Ethics is both a science and an art...It is necessary to effect in the treatment of the subject a revolution analogous to that which has taken place in the natural sciences...instead of beginning with theories and descending to facts, to begin with facts and to test theories by their fitness to account for the facts. But the moral facts...are not to be found in a stable external order; they are discovered in ourselves, they are found in moral experience. Hence, the richer our moral experience is, the more likely we shall be to possess an adequate inductive basis for our moral generalizations...[7]

In the richness of moral situations, Adler finds therefore the insight, stimulus and personal test of his proposed reconstruction. Experience would provide a continuous check on the accuracy and usefulness of his postulates and at the same time would provide for their amendment and development. Temperamentally, as those who knew him report, he seemed quite sure of himself, at least in his public conduct, and he tended to speak in an absolute mood. But he did not confuse this psychological security with verification. Indeed, his work may be taken as an invitation to philosophy. As he put it in describing the purpose of Ethical Culture, "We are to keep the ethical idea from petrifying no matter how sublimely conceived at any moment."[8]

At the same time, Adler was quite explicit about the conditions to be met by an ethical philosophy. Among other things, "a genuine philosophy of life can only be reached by the ethical approach...The great task...is strictly to carry out the idea of the independence of ethics...in the sense of independently investigating the problems peculiar to ethical consciousness."[9]

Adler was not a positivist, an emotivist or a utilitarian. Of course, he understood that ethics was conveyed by language, that moral judgment was embedded in custom and practice, and that consequences told the story of moral validity. But relativism and syntax failed to capture the urgency of moral reliability. Reductionist strategies would not do either. Ethics was neither psychology nor biology. For example, Adler criticized Kant's reliance on science. "In Kant, the Newtonian physics shines through the categorical imperative however sublimely proclaimed."[10]

There were indeed "ethical facts" to be found in ethical experience. Central among these was the reality and the realization of moral failure. The best of us could be a demon At the same time, the worst of us could still love his or her children. So moral incoherence was an ethical fact too. Yet another fact was the need for moral closure. Ethical experience did not permit indefinite postponement. Judgment, decision and action were inescapable.

A convincing ethical philosophy would, among other things, also have to take account of political and religious experience. History and tradition were ethical facts too. Thus, the ideas of soul and spirit which played so great a role in the traditions would have to find their modern counterpart. And the move toward equality, freedom and inclusiveness would call forth their own ethical reconstruction in a moral reading of democracy. The "evocative occasion," the moment in history, needed its moral response.

Ultimately, of course, specific prescriptions were necessary as guides to judgment and to action. So, Adler was given to mottoes just as Kant was given to maxims. But an ethical philosophy was not a moral cookbook. Instead, as C. D. Broad put it,

> You cannot deduce any particular argument from the general principle of the syllogism; but if any particular argument...claims to be valid, you can test its claims by seeing whether it does or does not have the formal structure required by the general principle. Kant would say, I think, that it is no more the business of ethics to provide rules of conduct than it is the business of logic to provide arguments. The business of ethics is to provide a test for rules of conduct...[11]

In other words, an ethical philosophy was not as such an ethical philosophy of life.

Adler knew that it was possible to add fact to fact and still fail to make moral sense any more than the mere collection of raw data can make scientific sense. As such, even ethical facts contain no organizing principle but only reflect the complications of human relationships. So, his task became the search for an organizing principle that would permit ordering the data and establishing moral priorities. He turned, intuitively, to the fact that men and women exhibit an evident desire for self respect and for the respect of others. In short, they do not want to be violated, and they want to be admired. At the same time, violation is a fact too so that evil is not simply an absence of good but a deliberate and active event.

It is out of the experience of self respect and violation that Adler reaches toward postulating the absolute worth of every individual human being. Of course, in a Christian civilization and in democratic societies this has a familiar ring. Indeed, one Roman Catholic critic takes Adler to task for not admitting that "the Ethical Rule works because it is a Christian rule in a Christian culture."[12] Adler, in reply, would no doubt acknowledge his sources. After all, that's what gathering ethical facts is all about. But he would also respond that genesis does not warrant monopoly and that the Greek, the Roman, the Jew, the Confucian and the Buddhist and countless others too might well claim a piece of the action.. Adler might also add that his project was not originality but the location and rescue of what is ethically valid from its theological, metaphysical and cultural accretions. Validity, finally is not grounded in the sources of principle but in its outcomes.

More seriously, Adler's postulate must, on his own grounds, face the facts, and the facts are that human beings are often meanspirited, selfseeking, given to anger, violent, hostile. The list of unworthy characteristics could probably be extended indefinitely. Moreover, in an industrial society we tend to make judgments of utility, of efficiency. In other words, we become exquisite calculating machines and set the price of everything, including human beings, as in wage labor and insurance settlements. To all of this, Adler is not blind.

> There are admittedly formidable difficulties in the way of attributing worth to human nature. The...most obvious of these is the existence of repulsive traits in human beings such as sly cunning, deceit, falsehood, grossness, cruelty...If the evil that men do revolts us, the so-called good in them does not give us the right to surround their heads with the nimbus of worth...[13]

On the evidence, then, it would certainly seem reasonable to conclude that any number of human beings are dispensable. But beyond the old story of the human propensity to do the wrong things, an industrial society has its practical requirements too. Men and women must serve social needs and a variety of economic purposes. Failing these, the world would simply come to a stop,, and suffering would only increase. How then treat persons as ends-in-themselves and what real and non-formal meaning could the postulate of worth possibly have? At first glance, then, the postulate will not do unless a dualism is reintroduced that isolates the practical from the ethical. Adler, as we know, is fully aware of this puzzle. As he says,

> The answer to the objection (the evident valuelessness of so many people) is that I do not find worth in others or in myself. I attribute it to them and to myself. And why do I attribute it? In virtue of the reality producing functions of my own mind...[14]

This leads him to work out a distinction between worth and value. The latter is merely empirical and historic, appropriately a matter of calculation and measurement. He then draws on his Kantian idealism to suggest that there is more than one dimension to human experience, as there is to the world itself. Of course the claims of the empirical world, in this instance the industrial world, cannot be dismissed. But they cannot be granted a monopoly either. There is a "supersensible" world too, although Adler is careful to say that it is a natural and not a supernatural world. Evidence for this dimension of experience arises just from the ethical facts which would have no basis in a merely utilitarian environment. Human beings evidently and persistently do desire self respect, look for social approval and want a "clear" conscience. Appeals beyond function are common enough and universal enough to suggest that value alone does not tell the human story, not even in an industrial world.

Adler goes on to add that whatever else the human being may be, he or she is also a rational being. Again the Kantian, he notes that one of the defining characteristics of rationality is autonomy, *i.e.*, that such beings give laws to themselves. Thus, it would be irrational and even absurd for contingency on the one hand and mechanistic determinism on the other entirely to shape the nature and conduct of a rational being. At that point, reason would be irrelevant and redundant. Of course, the world may in fact be wasteful and absurd. And so, cosmologically, rationality is a postulate too. In fact, as William James points out and as Adler would agree, "The widest postulate of rationality is that the world is rationally intelligible throughout after the pattern of some ideal system. The whole war of philosophies is over that point of faith."[15] For Adler, the human being's historic search for freedom and loyalty to ideal ends exhibits rationality, whatever its ultimate locus.

Finally, Adler shares with Kant a view of the "reality producing powers of the human mind." The moral imagination comes into play so that a new Kantianstyled question is raised: what kind of world emerges when such a postulate is taken seriously, and what kinds of future ethical facts are likely to appear?[16] But Adler is critical enough and honest enough to admit that a postulate is only that. Hence, worth is an "attributed" quality. In effect Adler says, let us try this out and see what kind of ethical philosophy can be built, what kind of ethical experience becomes possible. The mood is pragmatic.

Recalling his criticism of Kant and of Christianity, however, it is clear enough that worth is not axiomatically sufficient for an ethical philosophy. Adler had, after all, been highly critical of radical individualism, whether in religious or secular costume. The idea of the soul lacked social connection and was, as it were, directed only upward or downward. Kant's emphasis on the "good will" left men and women isolated from each other. Indeed, on Kant's formulation a world with one single member dutifully obedient to one single eternal and universal rule would be ethically possible and sufficient. And each single member in a multimember world could satisfy ethical criteria as an encapsulated monad. But, whatever its theoretical coherence, the absence of society could not stand the test of the ethical fact. Ethical experience was always social experience, relational experience.

Thus it is that Adler introduces the second postulate of his ethical philosophy, the notion of an "infinite spiritual manifold." It is described as an inclusive association of all unique individuals where each individual is necessary to all. The "manifold" has the distinct ring of the American motto, "*e pluribus unum.*" Thus, he socializes and democratizes the idea of worth. As he put it,

> No detached thing has worth. No part of an incomplete system has worth. Worth belongs to those to whom it is attributed in so far as they are conceived of as not to be spared, as representing a distinctive indispensable preciousness...morality depends on the attribution of worth...and worth depends on the formation in the mind of an ideal plan of the whole...let me say (it) more precisely, a rule of relations whereby the plan is itself progressively developed...[17]

Worth is thus the quality attributed to each person which legitimizes his or her inviolability and at the same time it is a certificate of membership in an ideal society of ends. So, it is both an individual and a relational concept.

From time to time, Adler had even spoken of developing a "science of ethics," not as a natural science, to be sure, but no doubt in the German philosophic tradition of *Geisteswissenschaft*. So his axiomatic style appears in form very much like the constructs we find in the other sciences. Functionally, axioms help us to connect data to prediction or, in ethics, experience to imperatives. For example, Adler offers three rules that express the "first principles of ethics."

> A. Act as a member of the ethical manifold (the infinite spiritual universe).
> B. Act so as to achieve uniqueness (complete individuation; the most completely individualized act is most ethical).
> C. Act so as to elicit in another the distinctive unique quality characteristic of him as a fellow member of the infinite whole.[18]

As we have seen, Adler himself had set the criteria by which his ethical philosophy was to be judged: is it coherent and inclusive; does it lend itself to usefulness in the world as it is; is it generalizable in that world; is it responsive to the person who is both rational and who experiences the "pains of being?" And it certainly seems that he comes close to success. For example, by socializing the concept of worth, Adler offers the basis for a philosophy of society that would integrate rather than fragment human beings. By reworking the notion of individuality, he provides a critique of the tendency toward conformism and a merely quantitative democracy. The inclusiveness of the spiritual manifold challenges traditional notions of "saved" and "damned" and, so to speak, democratizes heaven. It changes God from monarch into what Adler called the "multiple godhead." And by distinguishing worth from value without isolating them from each other he avoids the dangers of complacency and irrelevance.

Of course, it is possible to criticize Adler's axioms and his background cosmology. For example, once we are no longer trapped by atomism and sensationalism we may well be able to achieve Adler's ends without postulating a "supersensible" dimension. Nature, in other words, can be sufficiently rich to allow for the kinds of relationships he was concerned to defend. Ethical facts can be as available to empirical inquiry as other facts. As John Dewey put it,

> All generic scientific propositions, all statements of laws, all equations and formulae are strictly normative in character having as their sole excuse for being, and their sole test of worth, their capacity to regulate descriptions of individual cases...So far as scientific judgment is identified as an act, all *a priori* reason disappears for drawing a line between the logic of the material of the recognized sciences and that of conduct...[19]

The need for a radical separation between realms of experience disappears. Similarly, a naturalistic interpretation of the "rational being" and of "rationality" is available in the light of evolutionary biology. I might add that, once released from Kantian formalism, rationality need not be the only characteristic that legitimates worth. As a "loving being" it may well argued that the human being deserves to be inviolable. Indeed, Adler was aware of this possibility:

> ...if we desire an emotionally more appealing word than reciprocity, love rightly understood will answer, for love is the feeling which accompanies the consciousness of living in the life of another, of possessing and being possessed without loss of self ownership...[20]

As we shall see he expanded the meaning of "rational being" to include feeling and will.

Adler lives in a transitional moment between physics and biology. Although his background imagery can be challenged, an ethical philosophy is finally justified by where we are led by it. Thus, his assessment of the tendencies toward value in industrial society is surely to the point. In a world where manipulation has been elevated to high art, Adler's search for inviolability in the notion of worth is surely relevant. There are, in other words, interesting and useful consequences of taking Adler's ethical philosophy seriously. If the postulates of worth and the spiritual manifold are ontologically problematic, their utility for a theory of culture and of action are not. The mind may indeed be "reality producing" on any of several interpretations. The act, after all, is not unconnected to the mind and surely connected to events. What begins as the need to decide in advance of experience often turns out, reflexively, to have created the situation which ethical philosophy had postulated as already there.

Culture and Organization

For Adler, the ethical act is the most individualized act. Echoing his underlying romanticism, he rejects the reduction of ethics to legalism, to the judgments of the rational will and to obedience to universal moral law. "Become yourself" is the moral imperative. Moral rules, then, are to be judged by their relevance to biography. So a commandment like "tell the truth" becomes a feature of self development, as in notions like integrity, conscientiousness and the like. To become yourself implies too an emerging clarity about self, society and world. "Know thyself," the classic admonition, remains an ethical directive. Truthtelling, then, serves the purposes of individuation. Self delusion is, after all, an obstacle to moral maturity.

But the process of becoming yourself is not the lonely process of the hermit and the contemplative. Others too are becoming themselves, and between them and me there arises a reciprocal moral duty. As Adler put it, "We cannot save ourselves alone." So it is that he uses the imagery of organism:

> the organic idea is primarily a spiritual idea...Assume for a moment that this ideal were realized...a universe which would be constituted by the complete integration of its infinite *differentiae*...in such a universe each distinctively modified member would be necessary to all others as they to it...Reciprocal dependence is a telic idea...[21]

The language of organism and correlative terms like "organization" and "organ" become more and more frequent in Adler's work from the 1890's onward. They serve as metaphor for the ideal and thus situate the acts which we undertake as moral beings. "To ethicize and to organize," says Adler, "are synonymous terms." Once again, it is ethical experience that suggests the usefulness of the idea of organization.

In consequence of the increased differentiation of human society, what is called the organic nature of human relations now comes into view...Applying this conception to human society, we perceive the profound changes in the idea of morality which necessarily follow from it...The outcome...is that an act is moral not in proportion as it is standardized but as it is individualized, in the degree to which it is unlike other moral acts though based on the same fundamental principle, not in the degree to which it resembles them...[22]

Becoming yourself by helping others become themselves assumes the ultimate harmonization or perhaps better, the ultimate orchestration, of ontological, social and psychological reality. The development and indeed the survival of the whole as a whole needs the interaction of its distinctive members each doing his or her part. In that sense, the image of organism puts before us, too, a notion of irreplaceability which stands over against the interchangeable parts of mechanism. Adler's point is again pragmatic. An industrial society as we find it is not organic, although it is surely interdependent. Reconstruction begins from that fact and moves toward what such a society might become.

Organism is a scene of internal and not just external energies. No longer the bangings against and off each other in featureless space, the inertial motions of a billiardball universe, organism is ceaseless interactivity amid multiple relationships. There are no resting places and no places to disconnect. Indeed, disconnection is a symptom of moral illness. And unlike atoms in motion, organisms are changed and changing as they interact. Initially only speculation, a kind of moral poetry, organism comes alive for Adler in the social setting of industrial society. Every human being is to be unique and thus different in some essential way from all other human beings. Hence, my presence makes for a different organism, and were I not to exist, I would be missed. So, with organism I acquire both purpose and identity. Adler again is singing an Emersonian song.

Men are the pores of Nature and Nature cannot do without the perspirations. But in this grand body, each pore has a special function...We must not have cotton only, but cotton, hemp, flax, and mulberry; and every other weed in our *flora* will, no doubt, have its turn to be as famed a staple as the cotton pod is now. So that life teaches at every point the bifold lesson of assurance and humility. We cannot do without you; you cannot do without us...Only let each wear his own manners and milk not try to be brandy nor sulphur to be soap...[23]

To be in an ethical relationship is to "elicit the best in another and thereby in oneself," as one of Adler's mottoes put it. The criterion, then, is the development of another's uniqueness and reciprocally the development of my own. What might have been merely an ethical and secular restatement of the traditional notion of the immortal soul in the language of ideal and spirit turns out to be the guiding principle of social ethics by means of personal development. Distinctiveness leads to coherence and individuality and need not result in competitive anarchy. And departing from Adam Smith, individuality in action does not need the ministrations of an "invisible hand."

Behind Adler's romanticism there are, as usual, the ideas of the scholar and the experience of the reformer and the teacher. Organicism and the reciprocity of ethical relationships were the root ideas behind his redesign of the school, his counsel to the social worker and his reconstruction of religion. So, it makes sense for Adler to take up the idea of culture as the mediation between reality and ideal, substance and form. Culture has this middle status as process and bridge; it is the way that organicism and ethical experience connect. "Perfection is the end, culture is the means," as Adler put it in introducing his first Oxford lecture on culture. And he continued, "culture schemes...are projects intended to show to what degree...this absolute demand for fulfillment...can be achieved in a finite world...For culture is development...in a certain direction..."[24]

Latent in Adler's idea of culture is a notion of historic stages each of which imperfectly mirrors the ideal pattern and simultaneously leads toward its more complete realization. But imperfection remains the rule, and the ideal is never the real. So the "sensitive spirit" will never grow so enamored of any particular "scheme" as to lose sight of its partiality. Adler thus criticizes those who confuse the scheme with the ideal. He is thinking of classicists in education who try to replicate the "glory of Greece and Rome." He is also mindful of the way that the socialist image of a classless society or the Christian image of a messianic age is made absolute and even fanatical. Adler the idealist is also the imperfectionist.

Of course, Adler is literate in the social sciences too. So he is critical of their typical empirical usage which both misses out on the ideal and confuses the present situation with national and religious chauvinism masking as teleology. No doubt, he has in mind an earlier 19th Century anthropology which all too comfortably distinguishes the "primitive people" who came before us from western and Anglo-Saxon civilization which rightly owns the present. Living in a time when immigration was a major feature of American life, he is thinking too of the way that Native Americans, Irish and middle European immigrants are sacrificed to the needs and ambitions of their so-called betters, the immigrants who came earlier and now rule the country. Of course, there are advances in history, but the gulf between real and ideal remains. Legitimate pride in the achievements of nations and races does not warrant the claim of superiority. Moreover, the empiricist scientist looks to outward things, to artifacts and conquests, and so misses the point. As Adler put it early in his career,

> The very notion of culture...is an ethical notion...in the hierarchy of our faculties, the ethical faculty stands highest...We began with moral chaos, and we are gradually evolving cosmos out of chaos, separating the dry land from the sea and summoning out of their obscurity the stars which are destined to shine in our moral firmament...the value of this work is not much in the outward results achieved as in...the development of the creative faculty itself, in the soulpower which is liberated in the act of creation...[25]

The theme of an ethical culture is persistent.

Even as Adler was working out his philosophy of culture, he was engaged in an endless round of activity. The need for a "plan of the whole," therefore, was also a personal need. Adler was deeply troubled by what he saw around him. Public schooling was inadequate and often deadly in its triviality, its promise betrayed. Inclusiveness was deteriorating into "mobocracy." Labor was the victim of exploitation and profiteering. The crisis was everywhere and gave no signs of vanishing. The pattern of fragmentation, which John Dewey was to call "ragged individualism," meant the decay of community too. And all of this had its source in the failure of industrial society to understand itself. "The drift today is toward ever narrow specialism...Even government, the care of the life of society as a whole, is treated as a specialty."[26]

Where then could reconstruction begin? The one thing that Adler was convinced was under his control was himself. That, after all, was what it meant to be rational, free and autonomous. So "we are to regenerate society primarily by regenerating the one individual member of society for whom we are responsible."[27] And again demonstrating the consistency of his ideas over time, he echoed this nearly thirty years later when he said, "we must try to become cultured by working ourselves over."[28] Culture is thus not only an ethical mediation but a personal activity. It is not the "high culture" of appreciation, of aestheticism and dilettantism.

Organicism appears in Adler's description of culture as "a horticultural metaphor." Culture implies "a living thing...to be cultivated...a power of growth from within..." Genuine culture "aims to take hold of the whole man...to help him move in the direction of perfection..."[29] Individual action has its relationships to a universe of ideal ends. Only in that way could action have meaning. With this inclusive and ethicized definition of culture, Adler establishes his departure from elitism, from culture for the "cultured." Once again, he shows that he was an early member of the progressive's universe despite the idealist turn he gave to his thought. In the same mood, for example, John Dewey wrote in *School and Society*,

Unless culture be a superficial polish, a veneering of mahogany over common wood, it surely is this: the growth of the imagination in flexibility, in scope, and in sympathy, till the life which the individual lives is informed with the life of nature and of society. When nature and society can live in the schoolroom, when the forms and tools of learning are subordinated to the substance of experience, then shall there be an opportunity for this identification and culture shall be the democratic password.[30]

The capture of culture by the elite on the one side and by the social sciences on the other was deeply troubling to Adler. The former used it as an argument against the larger population; the latter used it to deny the relevance of normative values. The crisis, in other words, had its intellectual dimension which reflected the structure of industrial society. No doubt this view helps to account for the polemic vigor of Adler's style even when he wasn't preaching on a Sunday morning. His practice of drawing out the practices latent even in the most abstract of ideas was, no doubt, his way of demonstrating that even an idealist could stay in touch with the finite. And to the naturalists he was saying that even a philosopher could commit himself or herself in action.

Teleology

Culture for Adler, as we have seen, ultimately comes down to personal action, to the individualized and energetic act. It is, thereby, also a process of reciprocal interaction, since the individual needs other individuals not just for survival in the world of family life, politics and economics but for movement toward the ideal. But that suggests a problem for culture which Adler could not ignore. His first interest is to describe the moral agent but he must also explore the consequences for the individual of the moral failures of others. His social ethics relies on the fact that if I am to be cultured or nurtured, then I cannot accomplish that by myself. Thus, while it may be true that the one person for whom I am responsible is myself alone, reciprocity exposes me to moral dangers before which I am helpless and perhaps even blameless. At the same time that I attempt my moral work, I am dependent on the other to do his or hers. Yet, if he or she fails to do it, fails to act so as to elicit my uniqueness, my moral worth remains only an attribution. I cannot develop. To that extent, I am disabled from moral effectiveness and in turn ineffective toward the other.

The processes of culture, in other words, can move against the ideal as easily as for it. Thus, I can genuinely try for the best, at least subjectively, and yet turn out to be the worst just because of the failure of others. Again, we hear the words, "what we thought was civilization was not civilization." The persistence of moral frustration is in part a way of dealing with this problem, and in that sense is a reconstruction of the notion of sin. The permanence of a sense of tragedy is another. No doubt, Adler in his more optimistic moments could reply that the other cannot help but be shaped for the better by my action and so must respond more morally than before. But that is an act of faith, and as such another moral fact to be considered. But resistance is, after all, part of our moral experience too. Culture is thus a harsh and painfilled experience.

In a reminder of Kant's move toward the end of time in order to locate a final justice in things, Adler turns to the notion of purpose, of *telos*, to put an ethical culture into an ultimate moral perspective. The activity of the self and the dynamics of interaction are not adequate. By themselves, they are ultimately only processes. Indeed, this was the basis of Adler's criticism of Dewey and the other naturalists. But to be ethically effective, process must have both a direction and an end. We must be able to answer the questions: where is it all going, and where am I going?

> An end is what it is only in a society of ends...the concept, end, is a social concept, a systemic concept...[it] cannot be justified by means of the category of sequence, namely causality, but by means of the category of coexistence, namely reciprocity...Finality is as much a part of the aboriginal equipment of the mind as causality...[it] establishes a relation...of cooperation between different parallel and coexistent causal sequences...[31]

To be sure, Adler is attempting to rescue teleology from theology. And he is critical at the same time of a positivism that denies meaning to cosmic and moral purpose. But this was no mere sectarian or academic quarrel for him. Teleology was a biographical necessity at least as much as an ontological and epistemological problem. In this context, we recall that for Adler, "every ideal is intended to be a relief from some sort of spiritual pain..." And what could be more painful, finally, than to be convinced that our best efforts are ultimately pointless, and moreover that we often act in ways that, although morally intended, turn out to be selfdefeating because of the actions of others. Dealing with explicit conflict and direct opposition is, by contrast, easy. It is our dependence upon others that is the deeper problematic. For Adler, therefore, a "vision" of the end that embeds meaning and that ultimately resolves conflict is a moral requirement, yet another condition which an ethical philosophy must meet. The attempt to rescue teleology is motivated by a spiritual necessity.

Adler knew he was on even more shaky ground in the modern world. Darwinism had demonstrated that adaptation and time could accomplish what only looked like natural purpose. But, in a sense, he had been there before, as when he attributed worth to evidently worthless people. Once again, Adler goes against the spirit of the times when he puts the matter as a speculative and axiomatic notion. Of course, purpose cannot be demonstrated, and conflicting purposes are real enough. Yet, we still must meet the pragmatic question: on what present grounds can a moral future be created? In short, is there anything in ethical experience and in the ethical facts that could lead to a reconstruction of the *telos*? Indeed, there are realities which are opportunities for reconstruction. As it were, he turns for examples of such realities to the very sources of the problem of a natural teleology. Thus, there are any number of models of functional ends in biology and in society, models of purposive activity if not of some single cosmic purpose. To postulate a "society of ideal ends," then, suggests another location for the "reality producing" powers of the human mind. The spiritual manifold is thus a teleological reconstruction.

Reason too plays a role in justifying a teleological axiom. Adler, like Ralph Waldo Emerson and William James, includes feeling and volition within the capacities of a rational being. These are not merely arbitrary or capricious, nor are they unconnected to reason.

Is the rational equivalent to intellectual? If it be so, then feeling must be classed as irrational...And then the war will be on between the

> intellectualists or rationalists and irrational conceptions of life...An error
> is involved somewhere. It appears to consist in assuming that
> objectivity can be supplied only by the intellect, in overlooking the fact
> that feelings and still more the volition possess intrinsic controls and
> norms of their own...[32]

On the other hand, he notes that because the word "rational" would
only encourage a semantic quarrel, he prefers to use the word,
"spiritual" as the more inclusive idea. Whether that is any less likely
to stir semantic quarrel is, of course, debatable. Thus, when he speaks
of a spiritual manifold, he is alluding to a membership which is
characterized by the integrated capacities of reasoning, feeling and
willing.

It is these capacities that identify the culturing person, the person
who is a member of the society of ends. So, at the same time that
Adler offers a description of the spiritual manifold he locates it as an
ideal end, a *telos*. Facing from it back toward the world of ethical
experience, the agent now moves from "ought" to "is." Reciprocity
is not just interpersonal, historical and even political but cosmological.

> The true mark of culture is not to be found in any requirements or
> attainments...Even to the humblest callings may this idea be
> applied...When the shoemaker makes his shoe, the value (is in)...what
> the work teaches the worker...the fidelity of things and their properties
> which he learns while making it...It is possible to be an uncultured person
> as an artist and to be cultured as a shoemaker...[33]

Adler's teleology works as a criterion of active and existing cultures
but also as a source for the moral imagination. Without the ideal,
culture becomes only pseudoculture, a collection of the relics of what
were once living visions of perfection. At the same time, without the
ideal culture becomes pointless, literally endless, a process without
development. Adler's constructive logic issues in a completed
threefold pattern, the real, the ideal and the mediation between them.

Progress

With the idea of progress, Adler presents another reading, now an
historical reading, of culture and so conveys a sense of culture as
movement through time. Culture is a form of historical mediation
too. A romantic, he nevertheless still draws upon the Enlightenment
for moral and conceptual sustenance. Progress had been the basis of

the Enlightenment's historical analysis, its article of faith. Progress
had its tragedies, as when Condorcet wrote his extended essay on the
progress of human civilization in the shadow of the guillotine. It had
its ironies, as when a brutal disregard for the needs of human beings
was justified by the "progressive" ideas of social Darwinism. And it
had its low comedy, as when technological tinsel was welcomed,
especially in the America of the late Nineteenth and the Twentieth
Centuries, as the next step in human advance. Adler knew his history,
and he knew his America. In spite of his realism, however, he
remained a progressive.

A romantic tutored by the Enlightenment, Adler built on the
Eighteenth Century connection of democracy and progress.
Culture's end, the ideal thus became a democratic notion, a moral
politics. Again, Adler was building on ethical experience, the
American experience. But again, the ethical fact was both the motive
of reconstruction and its initiating substance.

> Standing at the terminus, I should say that one guiding thought for me
> would be continued interest in the progress of the human race...Progress
> means advance toward a society which shall more adequately reflect in all
> its relations the pattern of the spiritual world...

And he added in a footnote to this comment,

> That there is actually progress in human history it is impossible to prove.
> I rest my belief in progress not on the fact that it is demonstrable but on
> the moral pronouncement that it ought to be and that therefore it can be
> and must be...[34]

Progress, then, is not a descriptive but a normative idea. "The faith in
progress is not a scientific generalization...but a moral postulate...it
is...not to be inferred from the facts but...creates the facts which are to
justify it."[35]

Adler thought of progress as a series of "gradual
approximations" to the ideal. Admitting that history did not move
always and inexorably forward, he avoided the selfdeluding
historicism which had subverted the Enlightenment project.[36] Surely
aware of America's abuse of the democratic ideal, he rejected an
Americanism that was more rhetorical than real. Yet, he retained his
faith in the individual as the moral and political agent and in America
as the dream not yet fulfilled . As we have seen, when the individual
sets out to "culture" himself or herself, then reciprocally, he or she
will culture others. So, even if only a few individuals manage to

behave in accordance with the ideal, then to that degree progressive changes must follow.   And some few such individuals do in fact appear in history, although we may have no reason to expect them.   In a sense, Adler had embedded a theory of leadership in the idea of progress, and this was to appear in greater detail as a theory of vocational mastery.   He did not, however, identify leadership with a "revolutionary vanguard," as Marx and Lenin did.   The radical democrat was much too wary of authority.

But Adler hesitated fully to draw the conclusion that progress was inevitable.   No doubt he was concerned to avoid dismissal as a foolish optimist.   Philosophically, too, he remained under the influence of a Kantian ethical psychology.   Duty was to be done for duty's sake, and attention to consequences might endanger duty's moral credential. For Adler, however, the consequences that were morally problematic had to do with reward and punishment.   In other words, the idea of duty prevented morality from becoming mere prudence.[37]   But other consequences, the outcomes of reform socially and the development of the individual personally, were certainly morally relevant.   Duty was not blind to ethical experience.   The idea of progress thus reveals that Adler still struggled for an accommodation between his pragmatism and his ethical idealism.

With the idea of progress, Adler reveals himself as a radical democrat.   Ironically, he was in his personal life the Victorian gentleman and a member of New York City's intellectual elite.   Nor was he unaware of this irony, and so his reference to "spiritual pain" is in this connection both perceptive and autobiographical. Philosophically and morally, he rejected the notion that any group of human beings had special qualities that were forever denied to all others.   Indeed, his notion of individuation made him skeptical of any attempt at permanent categories and collective characteristics.   What was the social and personal truth of today would, in the move toward the ideal, become another and more inclusive truth tomorrow.

To be sure, at any moment some human beings would be better and others would be worse.   Nor was Adler blind to the class and caste consequences of deprived living.   He was not sentimental about the slums or about degrading labor.   These had their horrifying affects on personality and produced victims who were nearly incapable of being moral agents.   As victims, they were more likely to be corrupt and nasty than saintly.   But that was precisely the point of ethical experience, to stimulate moral action and thus to touch even the victim, making him or her less of a victim.   Reform, as we shall see, was not a change of social conditions but of persons.   The actual situation was impermanent, as all empirical situations were impermanent. Reconstruction is always a possibility.

> The idea of spiritual progress forbids leaving any man out of account...The kind of culture that I meditate...is not going to be the privilege of the upper class...real culture is possible for all...[38]

With the interpretation of progress as the direction of an ethical culture, we can find preliminary answers to Adler's question: what kind of ethical philosophy of life needs to be constructed in order to respond to spiritual pain? The answer that emerges is a radical democracy. The ideas of worth and the infinite spiritual manifold of Adler's ethical philosophy lead to practical images of human membership and human potency. They are the map of history as a progressive process, telling us where we have morally succeeded and where we have morally failed. The landmarks of the ideal and of the real are reciprocity and inclusiveness.

Education

Adler was a man of the academy and of the marketplace. He no doubt understood and sympathized with the question, "So what?" Ethical philosophy, the construction of coherent axioms and comprehensive ideal schemes are the stuff of intellect, no matter all the talk of action. Interesting they may be, perhaps, but again, "so what?" An ethical philosophy had to become an ethical philosophy of living. An idea had to show its credential by establishing, as William James put it, its "cash value."

Certainly an effective practitioner of the word, Adler knew that neither preaching nor intellect could lead reconstruction. Moral agents were not born but made; reciprocal relationships were had, not described. So it is that the ideal must find its practice in schooling. In other words, when culture is understood as an intentional activity, its name is education. Education is now a generic moral and social activity, not a preparation but a performance. Of course, it is found most explicitly in the classroom. But it cannot be left there. The world of politics, of business, of the law, is a schoolroom too or ought to be. Indeed, as Adler might put it, these surely teach but do not necessarily educate. Society itself, then, must be seen and judged from the perspective of education. The test of a society's moral credentials is to be found in how it, in all of its manifestations, educates its members.

Education, as we can see, carries a major burden for Adler. Of course, this is his Americanism again, the Jeffersonian notion of a literate and educated citizenry. Giving it his own accent to it, however, Adler, in effect, is restating the idea of worth as a form of practice.

> [W]orth or personality is not a static but a dynamic quality...It deals with man in his relations. It sees him a being essentially active whose very life consists in affecting the life of others. Worth, therefore, may be defined as that which provokes worth in others...Ethics becomes a science of reactions.[39]

But reactions can be automatic and visceral, or tutored and constructive. The new education is the move from the former to the latter, the move from mere reactions to "right" reactions.

Adler believed that his philosophy would ultimately stand or fall on its educational applicability. In practice, that is why he gave so much of himself and his energies to the schools he had founded and why the Ethical Culture Society was itself described as a "religious and educational" fellowship. Ethics cannot be judgment at a distance, nor can it be the appreciative contemplation of the good. A democratic ethics, moreover, cannot rely on the authority of the wise or on the revelation of the heavens. An ethics of worth is a progressive and progressively applied discipline for everyone, and not just for the talented few. So it demands the "having," and not simply the knowing, of experience. With that, we can understand Adler's location in the progressive tradition in yet another way. Experience becomes the point of curriculum, of lifecurriculum.

"Right reactions" or as Adler' sometimes put it, "right relations," is only a formula until its gets its content. So schooling must always be historical and biographical. Experience, then, is not narrowly conceived as simply "doing" anything at all with the stuff of reality. This was the satire of "learning by doing" which became a slogan of some of the later progressives and that troubled Dewey so much. The learned past and the disciplined present are both experienced.

The "world crisis" now returns as a pedagogical theme. Having reduced individuality to egoism and productivity to wage labor, industrial society is teaching an immoral lesson. And people are learning it, learning to value the isolated specialty, the extrinsic reward, the competitive arena. The need for counter-teaching is urgent. Failing that, politics exhausts energy without producing change, and schooling deteriorates into mere training. Of course, Adler like Dewey had genuine respect for proficiency and no use for good-natured bumbling. But any skill must interact with other skills and the skilled human being is known by the way he or she evokes complementary skills in others.

The school itself must be radicalized, must "educate reformers," as Adler had put it in describing the Fieldston Plan. So when he referred to his projects as "model" schools, he was looking beyond influencing other schools as such. As a model, the school would demonstrate the empirical and partial realization of the ethical ideal. It would be an experience and not just the preparation for future experience. But as a model, it would also be instrumental to the larger society. Again, the progressive theme is clear. Moreover, the school must depart from both traditional and modern practice, while reconstructing the virtues of both.

Summing up Adler's views, traditional education which initiates the newcomer into the rites of the tribe fails because it merely defends the status quo. Yet the process of initiation and a "reverence," as he put it, for the past are by no means to be dismissed. Technical education turns human beings into instruments that can fit the specifications of an industrial society. In that sense, technical education is the modern equivalent of tribal education. And yet, technical education also identifies and perfects the student's skill, and this cannot be dismissed. Humanistic and classical education founder on their elitism. They isolate getting and spending from the life of the good and the true and the beautiful. Thus, both economics and art are alike impoverished, and the human being loses a chance to develop his or her potency. Yet there is an appreciation of beauty and fitness in classicism that is indispensable. Only now it must be integrated with technique and practice.

What is needed, then, is a "new" departure in education, one that reconstructs the past and yet is responsive to the future. Schooling, like all of the rest of society, must be "ethicized." In other words, it must be shaped by a vision of the reciprocal connections of life to life and by the obligation of the finite to the "infinite" ideal.

Typically, Adler approached education from the side of social ethics. Thus, he criticized those who, inspired by the new psychology of personality and cognition, seemed to make individual development an end in itself. Yet again we hear the theme of reconstruction. The new psychology did in fact open development to enriched resources.

> [T]o what end do we educate...our answer to this question will depend on our philosophy and if our philosophy is ethical our answer must be distinctively ethical...reverence for the undeveloped human being...What is it that we are to revere in the child? Its spiritual possibilities, its latent

personality...We show our reverence for the child in the effort to personalize it.[40]

Adler, however, does not fall into the trap of focusing on ego development alone. The self is still the social self, and the personality is woven into the society.

An ethical education is also a democratic education, and this idea has several related implications. It follows, for example, that no human being can be dispensed with, can be dismissed as hopeless or, as we sometimes hear, as "ineducable." It follows, too, that no parent, teacher or administrator is morally authorized to give up on the human being, no matter what his or her condition. This is the active center of Adler's romanticism. Of course, he never forgot the distinction between worth and value. So he guarded himself against Rousseauian sentimentality which had appeared in the kindergarten movement and which was also to appear in a later progressivism. For Adler, in other words, the educator was not to surrender. He or she was a moral agent and so had an obligation to self that transcended the facts of the moment.

Indifference, surrender, despair are confessions of moral inadequacy, signs of the failure to pay attention to the moral meaning of frustration. As Adler put it,

> There is also another kind of challenge that in a way is even more taxing and searching: the silent appeal that comes from those who are spiritually dead; from those who are sunk in sloth or sensuality, or who waste their precious days in the pursuit of the trivial...and from the insensitive consciences of the self righteous and complacent...(a man) is bound to throw himself...as it were upon those who are spiritually numbed...All of which means that the task of edifying others involves continuous efforts at selfedification.[41]

Adler is practicing a certain dialectic philosophically and practically in the theme of reconstruction. He does not let us settle down to the single task except in the sense that the genuine single task is the interaction of all tasks. As soon as we attend to the social problem of specialism or of industrial labor we are driven to the individual. Committed to personal growth or self realization, we are forced outward to social relationships. Contenting ourselves with our successes with students who "want to learn," as we say, we must pay attention to those who are "spiritually numbed." Complacent in doing our duty to the "less fortunate," we discover an echoing numbness in ourselves and have to deal with self education and self development. Adler does not allow us or himself the privilege of serial attention now to this, now to the next problem. Of course, good societies make good people. Of course, good people make good societies. To start with one is to start with all. To solve one is to solve all.

In this massive task of reconstruction, Adler was by no means unwilling to use the fruits of scientific inquiry. Symptomatically, laboratory science played a significant role in the curriculum he designed for the Schools. He surely made use of modern psychology when, for example, he helped to initiate the "mother's society for the study of child nature" (later the Child Study Association) and when he worked to develop the teacher-training program of the Ethical Culture Schools (the Normal School). But empiricism, no matter how sophisticated, could never be enough. Ultimately, then, Adler's education was a "religious" education.

> [T]he things of earth are to be used as instrumentalities by which we are to become aware of the spiritual reality...[but] the disparateness of the physical world and the ethical universe should ever be kept in the foreground...Instead of seeking to explain, let effort go into utilizing. Let the world be used instrumentally for the purpose of verifying the existence of the universe.[42]

Adler's philosophy of education was finally a way of bringing worth and the spiritual manifold together with ethical experience in a constructive and intentional relationship. But education, no matter how generically understood, does not stand alone. Thus, the need emerges to consider vocation, personality and social reform as contexts for moving from ethical philosophy to an ethical philosophy of life. Setting out to respond to the existential problems of human living, the "spiritual pains," as he put it, Adler moves toward a comprehensive axiology and toward its import for practice. Setting out from practice, he moves to the reconstruction of axiology.

Notes

[1] Felix Adler, *The Reconstruction of the Spiritual Ideal*, New York, D. Appleton & Co., 1924, p. 33.

[2] Felix Adler, "Ethical Prerequisites of Personal Peace," address, December 16, 1917, p. 16.

[3] Adler, *Reconstruction*, pp. 13–25.

[4] For a discussion of these developments in the first half of the Twentieth Century, see Georges Friedmann, *Industrial Society*, edited by Harold L.

Shephard, The Free Press, 1955.

[5] Adler's concern and the terms in which he writes here are clearly Kantian. As Kant put it, "Man and every rational being anywhere exists as an end in itself, not merely as a means for the arbitrary use by this or that will....The basis of this principle is: rational nature exists as end in itself...." *The Fundamental Principles of the Metaphysics of Ethics*, translated by Otto Manthy-Zorn, New York, Appleton Century Company, 1939, pp. 45–46.

[6] Felix Adler, "In Commemoration of the Centennial Anniversary of the Death of Immanuel Kant," address, January 24, 1904, p.3.

[7] Felix Adler, "The Freedom of Ethical Fellowship," *International Journal of Ethics*, I, 1891, p. 25.

[8] Felix Adler, "The Purpose of the Ethical Movement," undated pamphlet, no page numbers, probably issued around 1890.

[9] Felix Adler, *An Ethical Philosophy of Life*, New York, D. AppletonCentury Company, 1918, p. 119.

[10] Adler, *Reconstruction*, p. 31.

[11] C. D. Broad, *Five Types of Ethical Theory*, New York, Harcourt Brace, 1930, p. 123.

[12] Samuel Frederick Bacon, *An Evaluation of the Philosophy and Pedagogy of Ethical Culture*, Washington, D.C., The Catholic University, 1933, p. 92.

[13] Adler, *An Ethical Philosophy*, pp. 91–92.

[14] Adler, *An Ethical Philosophy*, p. 121.

[15] William James, *The Principles of Psychology*, New York, Henry Holt & Co., 1890, II, pp. 676–677.

[16] Some years ago, inspired by this question, I tried to work out a modern version under the title, "Democracy and Duty," *The Humanist*, xxxv: 5, SeptemberOctober 1975, pp. 25–29.

[17] Adler, *An Ethical Philosophy*, p. 99n.

[18] Adler, *An Ethical Philosophy*, p. 117.

[19] John Dewey, "Logical Conditions of a Scientific Treatment of Morality," cited by Herbert W. Schneider, *A History of American Philosophy*, New York, Columbia University Press, 1946, p. 540.

[20] Felix Adler, "Fourth Lecture on Culture," Oxford, 1923, p. 16.

[21] Felix Adler, "The Relation of the Moral Ideal to Reality," *International Journal of Ethics*, XXI, 1911, pp. 3–6 *passim*.

[22] Felix Adler, "The Moral Ideal," *International Journal of Ethics*, XX, 1910, pp. 391–393, *passim*.

[23] *The Letters of Ralph Waldo Emerson*, edited by R. L. Rusk, New York, Columbia University Press, 1939, Six Volumes, III, pp. 404–405.

[24] Felix Adler, "First Lecture on Culture," Oxford, 1923, pp. 23.

[25] Felix Adler, "Ethics and Culture," address, January 9, 1888, pp. 8–12.

[26] Felix Adler, "First Lecture," p. 1.

27 Felix Adler, "The Recent Congress of American and European Ethical Societies in Zurich," *Ethical Addresses*, 3rd Series, 1897, p. 147.

28 Felix Adler, "Is Culture Compatible With Democracy," address, January 27, 1924, p. 7.

29 Citations are from the "First Lecture," pp. 7 and 8.

30 *Dewey On Education*, edited by Martin S. Dworkin, New York, Teachers College Press, 1959, p. 70.

31 Felix Adler, "The Problem of Teleology," *International Journal of Ethics*, XIV, 1904, pp. 275–276.

32 Adler, *An Ethical Philosophy*, pp. 131–132.

33 Adler, "Ethics and Culture," p. 5.

34 Adler, *Reconstruction*, pp. 215–216 and 216n.

35 Adler, *The World Crisis*, pp. 142–143.

36 See Howard B. Radest, *Humanism With A Human Face*, Westport, Conn., Praeger, 1996.

37 For a discussion of this theme, see Felix Adler, *The Religion of Duty*, New York, Mclure Phillips and Company, 1905.

38 Felix Adler, "Is Culture Compatible with Democracy," pp. 3–4

39 Adler, *The World Crisis*, p. 213.

40 Adler, *An Ethical Philosophy*, p. 295.

41 Adler, *An Ethical Philosophy*, p. 61.

42 Adler, *An Ethical Philosophy*, p. 134.

III

FROM COMMERCE TO CULTURE

Industrial Society

The marketplace as such is not ordinarily a philosophic theme these days. It is left to editorialists and political economists for comment. Where it is dealt with philosophically at all, it is resigned to what is miscalled "applied" ethics,[1] as if all ethics weren't applied or subsumed under questions of distributive justice. By contrast, a complex literature of social criticism developed in the nineteenth century. Emerson and Thoreau clearly responded intellectually as well as viscerally to the industrial condition. Political economy got its Marxist as well as its *laissez-faire* reading. A bit later, Thorstein Veblen, daring to be an ethicizing economist and pretty much dismissed by modern economists as an "institutional" economist, was to attack "conspicuous consumption." The "muckrakers" articulated the problematic ethics of America's commercial heroes. In religion, the Social Gospel tried to put the humpty dumpty of an incoherent and exploitive society together. Utopian ideas and not just utopian experiments were part of the tapestry of Adler's era too. A critique of industrial society in general and of American society in particular was not lacking. The problems of industrial society evoked questions of ethics and of meaning. Thus, they posed issues that were clearly philosophic and not just practical in nature.

Social criticism and radical ideology competed with a sense of the inevitability and desirability of industrial civilization. If imperialism and materialism challenged the credentials of the American dream, they also came clothed in images of progress. Yes, "things were in the saddle," but there were more and more things to go around and for more and more people. It is true that the "robber barons" fought for the dollar. At the same time, they were seen as unwitting agents of human advance. Looking back, it is easy enough to be reminded of Mandeville's "private vices, public benefits."[2]

In this setting, Adler develops his philosophy of industrialism and the reconstruction of its key terms: labor, productivity, mechanization, ownership and profit. Typically, he sees in each of these an opportunity for the moral ideal and no doubt would claim that he was "ethicizing" them. Although a radical, Adler was not a revolutionary. Industrial society was not only a fact. It was a new source of ethical experience. It opened new moral possibilities. Thus, Adler was not nostalgic for a return to some golden age, to a simpler and supposedly more humane past. Nor was he utopian, desiring a world that could never be. Dialectically, he worked with the opposition of worth and value to move toward the victory of the ideal. The tendency of industrial society to focus monomanaically on the "bottom line" was a stimulus to the moral imagination.[3]

When Adler founded Ethical Culture in 1876, he identified the "labor" question as one of the central moral questions of the era. In the 1890s it still remained at the top of his agenda. And at the end of his life, in the 1920s, his philosophy of vocation announced that he continued to struggle with the problem he had enunciated some fifty years earlier.[4] The "labor" question remained and had even gotten more difficult: the problem of integrating the "masses" as individualized human beings and as equal participants into a society that was becoming a mass society. The ascendance of industrial society dehumanized the owner, the manager and the laborer alike. Technical efficiency and the "profit motive" were the only things that mattered, at least in the public life. Indeed, President Calvin Coolidge was to make it official a few decades later with the immortal words, "the business of America is business." People were not the "ends *per se*" of ethical philosophy or the rational beings of democratic polity. The worker was a "hand," an adjunct to the machinery. The manager and even the owner used himself or herself as an instrument, a tool for some nonmoral good like wealth or fame.

The issue for Adler, then, is both ethical and economic. Drudgery has its spiritual impact. The boring labor of industrial society teaches the lesson of meaninglessness. It leads human beings to desperate alternatives. And the lesson is well learned. Once again, Adler turns to the "Great War" for its climactic message of the moral failure of industrial society. No doubt mindful of William James' 1910 essay on the "moral equivalent of war,"[5] Adler writes,

> Life is a great struggle to think well of ourselves. The greatest evil is neither poverty nor sickness but selfcontempt...do something, and at least for the time being you stand up large in your own esteem...The...desire to escape from the monotony of life is still one of the fruitful causes that leads to the exaltation of war...[t]he desire to break away from a commonplace existence...[6]

Thus the labor question is not only a matter of just distribution, as all too many moralists put it, but of moral psychology, philosophic anthropology and ontology. An increase of leisure and even a more equitable distribution of goods will hardly compensate for being treated as an object in the workplace and for agreeing that this is both necessary and good. Work itself has to be transformed. Here, above all, the move from value to worth is a moral necessity.

Monotony, even a well cushioned monotony, has deadly consequences. So industrialism makes violence in daily life and war in national life likely. Both technically proficient and emotionally appealing,

[t]he machine gun is the counterpart of the machine loom. Just as the substitution of machinery for hand tools...has made it possible for those who own the machine to oppress the laborer, so the creation of all this enginery of war has made it possible for the rulers...to throw back...the civilization which has been built up...Back of militarism is industrialism...The German emperor is a spokesman of...new markets...and the masses are full of the spirit of nationalism...[7]

Self-destroying labor and society-destroying war are joined by the third member of an industrial trinity, imperialistic nationalism. So global conflict is unavoidable if industrialism is unreconstructed. Its logic leads, ultimately, to the disappearance of the human being as a moral being.

The machine, then, is a disastrous ideal. With it, the tool becomes the master.

Take Henry Ford, for instance...he is working for efficiency in production...But he is not working for spiritual efficiency...It is true that the workers are paid better wages, but they are cogs in a machine...But what good is technical efficiency...if the men...are made more machinelike?[8]

Mechanism values efficiency and replaceability above all. The modern factory is but an enlarged machine, its parts including both machines and persons. Further, the industrial system is itself a collection of factories, as it were. So a series of increasingly complex and pervasive machines defines industrial practice. In that practice, worth has no place, and moral ends vanish before self perpetuating processes. Value, paradoxically, becomes the end, as in making money in order to make more money, building things in order to build yet bigger things.

The vices of an industrial system are competitiveness and specialism. Philosophically, competitiveness is justified by the notion of interchangeable parts. With that, a system loses nothing when it loses the losers. There is always another and identical thing to take its place. Failure in the market place warrants elimination. But elimination, according to *laissez faire*, is a good and not an evil, i.e., the inefficient producer deserves to be and ought to be eliminated. The language of competition only sounds neutral. It is, in fact, morally loaded. But, from an ethical standpoint, the disappearance of any member of the ethical universe is tragic and the deliberate elimination of any member is immoral. So a system that sets itself the norm of dispensability is *prima facie* morally dubious. Such a development of industrial society misses the opportunity of the ideal.

> Commerce with the finite...should be the means for man of asserting his infinite nature; work should be regarded...as an occasion for the worker to achieve the consciousness of his spiritual relations. And this finally leads to the ideal organic principle of reconstruction as the one which is here submitted as fit to replace the individualistic competitive, the collectivist, and the specialized altruistic or social service principle...In an industrial system...the personal relations will count above everything else...the supreme task is that of personalizing the depersonalized masses of mankind and their present depersonalized masters as well.[9]

Industrialism flourishes with the invention of the "division of labor." It is a method quite different from the differentiation of crafts and specialties that has been characteristic of the political, technological and economic life of many societies. In the industrial world each task is to be divided and further divided until all that remains is for the worker to make a single simple and repeated movement. The product as an understandable and aesthetic object vanishes. Industrial society thus marries specialty and mechanism to produce the division of labor. The outcome is specialism, which, leaving the assembly line, comes to shape all human activity. Industrial society thus captures talent and competence and reduces them to rote and routine performances. As it moves in this direction, it increasingly isolates the worker from his or her work and the work of any worker from the work of all other workers. The end of the process is the isolation of person and person as well as the fragmentation of the person into a hand, an eye, a muscle.

It was not necessary to wait upon the socialists or Karl Marx to find a critique of the effects of the division of labor. In fact, Adam Smith had warned,

> In the progress of the division of labor, the employment of the far greater part of those who live by labor...comes to be confined to a few very simple operations, frequently one or two. But the understandings of the greater part of men are necessarily formed by their ordinary employments.

> The man whose whole life is spent in performing a few simple operations...has no occasion to exert his understanding...He naturally loses, therefore, the habit of such exertion and generally becomes as stupid and ignorant as it is possible for a human creature to become...His dexterity...seems in this manner to be acquired at the expense of his intellectual, social and martial virtues...[10]

As industrial society moves toward specialism, the "spiritual pain" of meaninglessness becomes almost unbearable. Desperate people turn to anything for relief and for hope. War, as we have seen, is in Adler's view symptomatic of the consequences of the industrial move. A culture of violence and of amusements is the likely outcome. Indeed, were Adler a witness to modern terrorism and guerrilla warfare, he might well comment that these are both to be expected, and that they have, at least, the psychological validity of a self-defining act and a visible enemy.

But war is not the only disaster of industrialism. A never-ending process of dissatisfying satisfactions, a consumer society, is also its outcome. Adler, of course, is not an ascetic. He enjoyed theater, music and art, a good meal, a bit of wine, a joke. The virtue of industrialism is that it makes things like these more and more available to more and more people. The market is indeed a cornucopia. But when the goods of getting and enjoying come to dominate life, then a society has emerged which is antagonistic to the rational being, the spiritual being. Dignity and self respect, worth, in short, are sacrificed. As he put it long before a mass consumer society was visible,

> It must be admitted that there are times, the present is one of them, when among the struggling portion of the community the desire for wealth and comforts does seem to undergo boundless expansion...an insensate luxury prevails in the large centers of population...it seems as if the appetite for accumulation were only sharpened by every acquisition, not so much for the creature comforts which they can thus obtain as for the sake of the power which wealth concentrates in their hands, of the social prominence and prestige of which wealth has come to be the token...[11]

For Adler, the "cash nexus" is clearly dominant and self interest has become the moral as well as the economic rule. Yet, in his more hopeful moments, he sees this situation as only the symptoms of a "transitional epoch." For the first time in our ethical experience, wealth is a general and realistic possibility; so the "desire" for it understandably seems to have no bounds. But, he remarks that "enough is as good as a feast." The human being need not be condemned to the insatiable, need not be only a competitor and only a consumer. Adler thus rejects the tradition of Macchiavelli and Hobbes, the tradition of the human being's allegedly incorrigible drive for things and power. By contrast, Adler is still the classicist and squarely in the Aristotelian tradition of moderation in all things. The human being is indeed a social animal and remains so even under industrial conditions. Adler's interpretation of the moral opportunity of industrialism, the widest possible interdependence, is thus a modern reading of the classical tradition.

But he is not alone nor, as recent developments tell us, can he be accused of being a "mere" moralist. In Adler's own time, and no doubt part of his background awareness, an influential school of French sociology led by Emile Durkheim read modern society in a similar way.

> Thus, altruism is not destined to become...a sort of agreeable ornament to social life...How can we really every dispense with it? Men cannot live together without acknowledging and consequently making mutual sacrifices...Every society is a moral society...Thus, it is wrong to oppose a society which comes from a community of beliefs to one which has a cooperative basis, according only to the first moral character and seeing in the latter only an economic grouping. In reality, cooperation also has its intrinsic morality.[12]

Adler's "Businessman's Group," consisting of members of the Ethical Culture Society, provided him with examples of the economic effectiveness of industrial and commercial cooperation, as did his own efforts at labor mediation. For us, recent developments in industrial reorganization, in management theory and practice, also provide an empirical justification for Adler's rejection of the notion that the human being is motivated only by self-interest.[13] Altruism, too, has escaped the bounds of sentimentality and, indeed, has even found its neo-Darwinian justification in the notion of species survival.[14] And finally, stimulated by feminist insights in philosophy and psychology, an ethics of "caring," mutuality and interdependence develops as a moral alternative to individualism and legalism.[15] So Adler is still a realist, even perhaps a prophetic realist.

Adler must contend over and over again with the view, current in the American of his time, that "profit" and self interest were the only reliable and realistic ways of getting things done. Rationalized by free market theory, the rhetoric of profit was met primarily by a Marxist and socialist opposition. But neither the free market nor socialism satisfied Adler. Both were addicted to a "labor theory of value,"[16] both made the "means of production" the central fact of political economy, and both separated human beings along the lines of economic class. In other words, both market theory and socialism perpetuated the moral disease of industrialism, the sacrifice of worth for value. As it were, the reformers only touched the edges of the problem here and there; they were doing piecemeal reform.

An ideology of competition and conflict, whether socialist or *laissez-faire*, is a moral failure, a failure in particular to seize the opportunity of industrialism for the sake of the moral ideal. Ever the realist, however, Adler supported the nascent labor movement of his day, cooperated with civic and social reformers, and worked to improve the conditions of the poor. But he challenged even these, and even his own efforts at times, for lack of a philosophic foundation, a "plan of the whole," as he had put it in describing the "spiritual manifold." All around him, he saw evidence of "provisionalism,"[17] and that would not do.

Marxism, moreover, embeds a fundamental moral error in its ideology of class warfare. It sees the ethical ideal as only an "epiphenomenon" of productivity. For Adler, this is to put things in precisely the wrong order. To be sure, it can be pointed out that he misreads Marx, although not the Marxists and, a bit later, the Leninists of his time. Clearly, as Erich Fromm notes, Marx was primarily a moralist.[18] Indeed, the then President of the Ethical Society, the Columbia economist E. R. A. Seligman, made a similar point in *An Economic Interpretation of History* in 1902. With his comment that "spiritual" considerations influence economic behavior, Seligman is, no doubt, reflecting Adler's influence and criticizing him at the same time. As Morton White sums it up,

> in the chapter on "The Spiritual Factors in History"...Seligman dealt with what he thought was a misdirected objection to Marx's point of view...Seligman said, "It would...be absurd to deny that individual men, like masses of men, are moved by ethical considerations...all progress consists in the attempt to realize the unattainable, the ideal...(but) purely ethical or religious idealism has made itself felt only within the limitations of existing economic conditions...[19]

As usual, Adler has both a theoretical and a practical agenda in mind in rejecting both *laissez faire* and socialism for failing to reflect ethical experience. All too often, the so-called limitations imposed by economic conditions become an alibi for refusing to engage the process of reconstructing society. Budget balancing is a perennial excuse. Frustration with reform and the partiality of its successes tempt us to retreat to an illusory realism. Adler's inversion of the Marxist thesis, then, is a pragmatic and not simply an intellectual criticism. Economics, like politics, must submit in the final analysis to the criticism of ethical principle.[20] "We should try," Adler writes, "to substitute living labor, i.e. development toward a society of ends, for dead labor, i.e. mechanical, repetitive labor." In a similar way, Georges Friedmann sums up the analytic literature on this point,

> [T]here are considerable differences between different mechanized tasks...It is untrue that *in itself* the machine suppresses all joy in work. It is the conditions imposed by a narrowly technicist rationalization...which widen the gulf between the worker and his mechanized work...separating the worker from all occupational thought...maintains this gulf. It is also aggravated by the unsatisfactory social relations between workers and supervisors within the firm...[21]

Realistically and ideally, the industrial situation is deadly in the effects of routine but hopeful in its invitation to everyone to be included in the world of work. Searching out the "joys" of labor, the experience of productivity within the industrial condition, is then the heart of Adler's philosophy of vocation and, as such, the key to industrial reconstruction. In a way, then, Adler too has a "labor theory of value," but the energies that are mixed with the stuff of nature are ethical and not economic, ideal and not empirical.

A Theory of Work

Adler is quite explicit about his goal: to reconstruct the classical and the religious notion of vocation in ways consistent with modern secular practice. He announces it as the ultimate step in his lifelong exploration of the "labor" question.

> Vocation...invariably means related to the spiritual end of life. A profession or occupation becomes a vocation when he who follows it seeks to respond to the *call* of the latent spiritual possibilities in his fellow men...[22]

Behind this brief comment are his experiences, his ethical experiences, with the printer's cooperative, the Workingman's School, the relationship with Samuel Gompers and the early days of the Cigar Makers Union and later the AFL, and his role as labor mediator. Ethical experience, as Adler would put it, has led him to vocation.

With industrialism comes a radical change in the ways human beings earn their bread and spend their time. But the new situation is not matched by a new ethic. So old moral habits are still in play but are found to be less and less useful. Little wonder, then, that ethics has become an abstraction and that, in practice, the norms of commerce have become pseudomoral norms as well. An ethical theory of work, then, is urgent. Characteristically, Adler turns to the historic record and picks up the traditional notion of the "calling." As R. H. Tawney describes it,

> *Laborare est orare.* By the Puritan moralist, the ancient maxim is repeated with a new and intenser significance. The labor which he idealized is not simply a requirement imposed by nature or a punishment for the sin of Adam. It is itself a kind of ascetic discipline imposed by the will of God and to be undergone not in solitude but in the punctual discharge of secular duties...It is a spiritual end, for in it alone can the soul find health and it must be continued as an ethical duty long after it has ceased to be a material necessity...[23]

Adler, like the Puritans, also gives "vocation" a decidedly American accent. Salvation is to be found neither in status nor in ideology but in doing the work of the world Thus, with both tradition and Americanism as his sources, he arrives at vocation's industrial reconstruction.

Adler was not a Luddite. Far from rejecting the division of labor, he asks how it can contribute to the move toward the ideal. The machines and the machinery have to be converted, as it were, and not destroyed. With this moral strategy in mind, Adler points out that industrial society evokes many new skills and different talents and distributes their practice more and more widely among people. The division of labor without the leavening of an ethical philosophy, however, produces only dehumanizing monotony. But under a technological and democratic inspiration it also promises an increase of competence and effectiveness. Human powers can be released of which earlier societies could hardly dream. If ethics is the "science of right energizing," then here is indeed a scene of glorious energies. An industrial civilization could thus become much richer ethically than a pastoral, a rural or a feudal one. The interdependence of men and women which is modeled by the division of labor can be "organized," can be ethicized. "Society," Adler writes, "is sometimes called an organism. This is grotesquely untrue...Its members are at war with each. Society is by no means yet an organism...it is to be made such..."[24]

Ethical possibility, as usual, needs intentional activity, and activity needs direction as well as end. Here, the profession and the professional offer Adler an empirical model for a more generalized reconstruction of work. Taking a clue from the way he talks about them,[25] it is clear enough that ethical experience teaches us the distinction between profession and industrial labor. Certainly any profession includes repetition and dullness, but while these may on occasion be resented they are not, in themselves, drudgery. The moral and intellectual characteristics of the profession make even routine acceptable because understandable as to means and ends and because autonomously determined. The profession is not simply a choice of work but a continuous choosing while at work. A profession has a known and visible *telos*. It also has a tradition and a code and enjoys legitimate social recognition. A profession is, in other words, technical, ethical and historical all at once. By contrast, the industrial worker is a slave of the clock but has no sense of time except as duration. As the worker remarks, "I put in my hours." In this context and unlike labor, a profession's long preparation, repeated rehearsals and mechanistic tasks may be fatiguing but are not debilitating.

Where the qualities of the profession replace those of the "job" or even of the "career," the "cash nexus" becomes less central as motivation. Living is not reduced to earning a living. And this, as industrial research has consistently shown, is as true of the skilled craftsperson. Indeed where the "job" replaces the profession, where autonomy is subverted by hierarchy and skill by mechanization, the financial reward does in fact become the primary motive. This, as we know, is the move toward "bureaucracy" symbolized by complaints about "red tape" and meaningless paper work. Tasks are standardized. Routines overtake professions like social work, teaching and the law and today threaten to overtake medicine too.

Typically, the managerial reformer only addresses the superficialities. Thus, all kinds of work are given the professional label even where *telos*, autonomy and control of the mean-ends relationship are lacking. Too often, "human relations" techniques, like the promiscuous award of "job titles," build an illusory world of industrial reform. But these are finally only strategies of pacification and lack the features of self respect, autonomy and interdependence that were Adler's cues to reconstruction. None of this, by the way, escapes the newly crowned "professional." Thus efforts to unionize white collar workers and professionals and, more recently, nonprofit and government employees exhibit both the loss of autonomy and purpose and the consequent focus on economic motivation. In a further validation of Adler's insight into vocation, efforts to remake the job are as typical just about everywhere today as the reduction of professions to mere jobs and as the use of manipulative techniques. We are, in other words, still in the transition that Adler had described as it was making its first appearance. Symbolically, these efforts at job reform on all sides confess the inadequacies of viewing the division of labor as a neutral or even a beneficent technology.

Industrial society does in fact move in the direction of a more inclusive and interdependent structure than all prior societies. Durkheim had, of course, put the theme in the context of social solidarity.

> This is what gives moral value to the division of labor. Through it the individual becomes cognizant of his dependence on society; from it come the forces which keep him in check and restrain him. In short, since the division of labor becomes the chief source of social solidarity, it becomes at the same time the foundation of the moral order.[26]

A vocation appears, however, only when the specialty both builds and is built by the ethical "personality" and when it moves toward an interrelationship of personalities and not just functions. Occupations are typically opportunistic, and extrinsic rewards are their motivation. As usual, Adler is concerned to criticize the reduction of person to object. For him, industrial society is only latently a genuine moral advance. As such, it is a promise and a threat. Solidarity is not enough and would not insure an ethical society. Interdependence can mean anything from freely entered relationships to job slavery. Cohesion is, by itself, not morally determinate.

"The keynote of my ethical system," Adler says in 1923, "is the supereminence of vocation."[27] A bit earlier, he had written, "my task is an ethical classification of vocations..." Then he suggests a preliminary typology which, unfortunately, was never completely developed. He begins with the theoretical sciences and their "practical" counterparts where "work in factories, mines, and also in the fields is to be regarded as the executive side of theoretical science." He adds the historical sciences and the vocations of the artist, the lawyer and judge, the statesman and the religious teacher.[28] Adler is careful not to isolate the profession from the trade, the academy from the marketplace. But these are collective names for legitimate specialties which can only do their job if they are not reduced to each other. When organized by a unifying ideal and supported by interactive practices, however, the "spiritual pain of the divided conscience" can be eased if not eliminated.[29]

Vocation has its products too. It is a vehicle for the emergence of moral character. So what is made and what is done must, as it were, be ethicized too.   By contrast, left to the standards of an unreconstructed commerce, the product is seen only as an economic good and the producer only as an economic instrument. Product and process are quite literally alienated from each other. Their connection is the purchase price and the wage, a nonpersonal and quantitative connection. Ethicized, the maker, the things that are made and the way they are made are not strangers to each other "[T]he true test of the cultivated man...is how...[he] behaves in his counting room or factory or office or studio..."[30]

Dialectically, the producing personality is inevitably in relationship with other producing personalities.   Ethically, that relationship is not merely utilitarian, a relationship of person and object. A vocation, in other words, is identified by the integrity of the skills it demonstrates and by its place in a society of skills. It is the labor counterpart of the "spiritual manifold." As Adler puts it,

> Specialism we must have, but culture is to be the cure, the antidote to specialism...vocation so arranged that your vocation whatever it is shall no longer be pursued narrowly...but so that you shall lay significance on the effect you produce on corelative specialists and the effect you get from them in return. The ethical relation is the cross relation...[31]

Recalling that, for Adler, "the ethical act is the most individualized act," the relationship of producer and product is aesthetic, and it is difficult to know whether aesthetics is to be ethicized or ethics is to be aestheticized. In any event, they are intimately connected. The model is ultimately the art and the craft, now reconstructed in an industrial matrix.   In the empirical world, the product reveals the talent nurturing and nurtured by all other talents.

Drawing a line between labor and vocation, Adler knows how easily he can be challenged by the so-called realists, the economists, politicians, engineers and managers. As with Marx, however, he points out the conceptual and psychological limitations of *"homo economicus."*   Indeed, the reduction of the human being to an economic animal was not so much the intent of classical *laissez faire* theorists as the sloganeering of popularizers and opportunists. Adam Smith, as we know, was the moralist as well as the political economist. And, as Morton White points out, John Stuart Mill was careful to make clear that the notion of *homo economicus* was essentially methodological.

Political economy considers mankind as occupied solely in acquiring and consuming wealth and aims at showing what the course of action...would be...if that motive...were absolute ruler of all their actions...[But, Mill denies that any] political economist was ever so absurd as to suppose that mankind are really thus constituted...[32]

A bit of self examination would also show that it is indeed a factual and not an empty claim to say that "man does not live by bread alone." Formal inquiry into human motivation corroborates autobiography. Satisfaction is more complicated and varied than is captured by a model of self interest and extrinsic reward. Failure to satisfy in this more complete way what Adler identifies as "spiritual pain," has already had its outcomes in social violence and pathological consumption. Today, we might add that it has its outcomes in addictive behavior and mental illness as well. Experience continues to corroborate ethical philosophy.

Adler avoids romantic clichés like the "well rounded" personality. Competence calls for the mobilization and focus of energies. The issue is not specialization but specialism. To do anything well demands dedication, mindedness. "But neither for women nor men is it possible to follow two vocations at the same time...every real vocation is exigent and becoming more so..."[33] Failing the development of skill, we are left with incompetence on the one hand and gameplaying on the other.

Just because an ethicized industrial society is built on the unique talents of the individual, the need of person for person grows. A sense of the irreplaceability of the other, a moral sense, is realistic with

the increased necessity of restricting oneself to a limited field in order to achieve anything like...mastery and the inevitable fractionalizing...which is the consequence...In the idea of outreaching radiations of interest and of the give and take relation there is the promise of liberation from the narrowness of specialism without the calamity of dilettantism..."[34]

Vocation is not the privilege of an elite or of those few who are called by God. Echoing Martin Luther, who put the matter in theological terms, Adler writes, "Ethically, every human being is called..." So, in practice, all occupations must be transformed. Work is to have its intrinsic values.

Even as Adler is looking toward some ultimate reconstruction of labor, he is mindful of the actually presented problems of his time.

Again, he reveals the move back and forth between ideal and real. This is well illustrated by his discussion of a "just" wage.

> I have long since given up the attempt to establish an equation between the just deserts of the worker...and wages...The proportion between work done and income received will have to be based on a totally different principle...I mean...sustentation and not remuneration...The just principle is that which sustains the worker at the highest possible pitch of (vocational) efficiency...The reward of work...is or must be in the work itself.[35]

Adler is critical of capitalist and socialist for making a crucial conceptual error. They both use the rhetoric of egoism. Even the more radical reformers lack a sense of transcending purpose. The debate everywhere is between the possessors and the dispossessed over possession itself.[36] Adler knows that the "haves" and the "have nots" are in conflict. He was not opposed to tactics like strikes, and he was not a pacifist. But he also recognizes conflict's peculiar dangers in an interdependent industrial society. Human beings could be far more destructive now than ever before. Under these conditions, one world war, he seems to be saying, is one too many.

Frustration and failure are part of Adler's philosophy of vocation too. Thus, each vocation has its vice, the temptation of "a kind of behavior the very opposite of that prescribed by (its) particular ethical function..."[37] For example, the judge and the lawyer are to be the "teachers of justice." The vice would be a blind conservatism, the refusal to admit that justice evolves. The teacher, for example, is reduced to the administrator or trainer. When, moreover, the judge fails to "awaken all men to the fact that society shares the guilt," he or she reveals the vice of his or her vocation by missing out on the social relationship, the evocative relationship.

Adler is thus the idealist without illusions. He does not assume that moral pronouncement will be followed by moral change. There is hard work to be done and resistance to be overcome. The assembly line will not easily be transformed.

> The relief of industry from the blight of drudgery...may perhaps be found in the following directions: 1. combination of agriculture with industry; 2. the pushing of automatism further and further along...; 3. the classing of monotonous labor...as excessively onerous labor...shortening hours...so that a man or woman shall be expected to work at mere machine tending only a limited number of hours...; 4. the development of

new finishing industries, crafts and other occupations in which the personal element is the predominant factor.[38]

Adler notes, in this connection, his debt to socialism. But he points out that its solution "despairs" of redeeming the "worker through his work." Instead, it leaves work as routine and mechanistic and urges increased time for family and leisure. His idea of vocation is a way of saying that "soul-less drudgery" is not a morally appropriate payment for wealth and leisure.

A striking instance of Adler's pervasive sense of the relevance of vocation is his description of motherhood as a "new" vocation. Again, industrialism points the way, for it has transformed the family and so made the mother's work a more complex and demanding task, indeed an "executive science," in Adler's typology of professions.

> Now motherhood is, or at least is in the way of becoming, a true vocation. It draws upon various sciences, on chemistry, physiology, on psychology, on the applied arts, on applied ethics...and beside, since the family is the foundation of the state and the right ordering of the state reacts upon the family, the wiser [view of] motherhood implies active participation in public life...[39]

Not the least of Adler's motivations is the need to deal with the increasing presence of women in the marketplace. Practically, and not just theoretically, it was necessary to recognize the social role of motherhood, or else women would either leave it behind or else be excluded from society. They would, in either case, not be participants in the realization of the ideal.

Stimulated by the problem of meaningless labor, Adler thus moves toward a general theory of vocation. Indeed, industrial society is a progressive move in human history. But the condition of the worker, the "labor" question, is the most visible and demanding instance of the need to transform work from an economic into an ethical phenomenon. Every public activity has to be made into a vocation.

Given to the motto, Adler sums it up in a Kantian mode as "So work that the work of the world shall be better done because you have worked in it."[40] His insights and his examples, however, are not plucked from thin air. Among his confidants were bankers and lawyers, factory owners and factory workers, business men and labor leaders. From them he gained a practicing knowledge of the problems and possibilities of the industrial system. Consequently, Adler's views ring true even today. His hero was neither Horatio

Alger nor the bemuscled worker of Soviet realism.   Instead, he
includes all persons in a reconstructed industrialism seen as the
contemporary "occasion" for realizing the moral ideal.

A Sense of History

Humanity is a type of ideal form.   Experience is its instantiation
in a moment of time.   Thus history becomes a crucial dimension of
Adler's thought.   Unfortunately, he did not elaborate a philosophy of
history, but his ideas can be pieced together from references in his
texts and addresses and from his descriptions of school curricula.   It is
clear enough that he does not believe that history is simply a lesson
book that will help us avoid the mistakes of the past.   He understands
the persistence of human stubbornness.   Above all, as a radical
pluralist, he respects the necessities of particular histories and
biographies.   Difference is morally valuable and sameness is ethically
suspect.   The past serves and is not merely to be overcome in a burst
of modernist enthusiasm.

Adler puts a critical history at the center of the school
curriculum.   Without it, education is shallow and only of the moment.
And, most significant in an industrial society, people have histories.
Machines, on the other hand, do not.   They only have specifications
and performance records.

Adler's sense of history is also a response to both left and right
Hegelians.   "Whatever is," is not necessarily "right."   Thus, he
rejects a Marxian determinism which predicts the inevitable victory of
one class over another.   He finds Spengler's "decline and fall," the
notion of the automatic ascendancy of one civilization over another,
equally suspect.   As against historicism, however, technology which
seems to live in an eternal present lacks an evolutionary perspective.
Yes, Henry Ford might proclaim that "history is bunk," but the
"problems of men" come clothed in antecedents.   Of course, he
respects the integrity of the present, any present.   But the present is a
moment between past and future.   The ethical task, then, is to ethicize
time, to seize the present for the sake of the future.   But the moral
strategy does not permit ignorance of where the present came from.
So, for example, while reflecting on what was to become the
"Fieldston Plan," he says,

> What should be the aim of history teaching? History should be taught so
> as to contribute to the evolutionary idea...The question that the Sphinx
> asked is nothing else than, Man what art though? ...Now history is the

record of the answers that have been tried... And every one of these answers had a partial truth in it and therefore the civilization which corresponded to it survived for a time; and it was radically false and therefore every civilization thus far has perished...[41]

The historian who does not locate the "ethical" element, does not try the riddle of the Sphinx, has missed his or her vocation. He or she becomes merely a specialist. Of course, history is studied as an academic discipline. But it is lived as ethical experience.

Revealing again that they lived in the same progressive neighborhood, Adler's sense of history comes close to John Dewey's notion of "funded experience." It is, in Dewey's metaphor, a kind of extended social laboratory. Adler is less "scientific." For him, history presents models of the ideal and its projects. But both men understand the moral uses of history, and both see it as describing the tension between the uniqueness of a history and the commonality of human history.

With a sense of history, Adler challenges the advocates of mere modernity for whom the present is all that really matters. It is a sense of history that helps us distinguish between vocation and job, that tells us we are in the process of reconstruction. The vocation has a history; the job has technical description. Again, Adler is most explicit when he addresses the role of history in education.

I want the young man whom I am educating to be in touch with his vocational ancestry...And in order that he may acquire this point of view, I would unroll before him the great panorama of the commercial and industrial people from antiquity to the present day...The story must be told...with color and movement and life...He must realize the good they have done...But he must also be taught to see that...trade went its way...through human affairs...regardless of the effects it produced on other great human interests...because this was so, there is another seamy side to commercial history...The student must not be allowed to overlook the favorable side...but he may not overlook the evil [either].[42]

In so far as Adler insists on ancestry and antecedents, he knows that he too will become an ancestor. He too will be surpassed as a vehicle of partial truth and as a perpetrator of evil. Our inadequacies are not merely superficial or only the outcome of a failure of the "good will." Thus Adler's notion of "frustration," which arises from the gulf between the real and the ideal, acquires yet another empirical meaning in history. A sense of history is also a sense of the future. Looking backward we judge and respond. Looking forward we are judged and responded to. Connection, organism, is a temporal as well as a spatial metaphor.

A sense of history reflects the activity of human consciousness as intention. Adler is clearly kin to what later evolutionary biologists mean when they say that the human being is "evolution become self conscious."[43] A special type of consciousness is involved, however, a cultural or organic consciousness. Vocation, in this evolutionary perspective, is culture's instrument. It is of course an exhibition of excellence but it is an exhibition of relationship too.

> [W]hat is my own specialty to give me? Is it just this particular knowledge or skill? No, I am to become more aware of my work by putting forth values...Hence it follows that what I am to get from other specialties...is the movement of life in them...the object of culture is to identify oneself...with humanity...Practically, this would mean a great emphasis on history...each of the great branches of human activity is related to all the others; and culture...is inclusive of all...[44]

Again, this reminder of Dewey's thought is worth noting. As he remarks, "It is through occupations...that mankind has made its historical and political progress...In education terms...occupations in the school shall not be mere practical devices...[but] points of departure when the child shall be led into a realization of the historic development of man."[45] The common thread of progressivism unites Dewey and Adler, although one was an instrumentalist and the other an idealist. The pragmatic and romantic intention thus transcends ontology. So, although Adler criticized his Columbia colleague as a "provisionalist," there is a good dose of idealism in Dewey's thought. Dewey, in turn, found Adler's idealism blind to the moral and political promise of the natural sciences. But they were closer than they were prepared to admit.

As a culture, industrialism has given the talent and the specialty a high profile, and so the imperfections of other cultures, their failure to make connection inclusive, need not be its fate. In fact, a reconstructed industrialism has a unique opportunity to remedy history's failures by teaching the lesson of organicism. That is its ethical justification, even its mission. Of course, it too, like other cultures, will fall short of the ideal, will have its vices. Nevertheless, it offers the opportunity for vocation to reconstruct history, to be progressive.

Adler extends his pluralism to nations as well as to specialties and persons, and so hints at an "organic theory of nations." Motivated by the failure of the League of Nations to be a "society of mankind," Adler point out that,

> every nation represents a certain type of human civilization...The society of mankind is the organization in which these different types are to be assembled...each playing its functional part in evoking from the others their best possible contributions to the ulterior perfection of civilization...[46]

Vocation, generalized, teaches the virtues of variety. Adler's patterned way of thinking suggests an organic theory of international relations. A nation, too, has its vocation.

As usual, Adler's motivations are never singular. So his concern for a theory of work is coupled with his concern with conformity. Differentiation as a model of the moral ideal challenges the reduction of equality to identity and of traditions to mere commonality. As he notes,

> We have dwelt too long upon the cosmopolitan ideal of the likeness subsisting underneath the differences...We must insist...on respect for the differences themselves, on the right of men and of nations to be unlike ourselves, on our obligation not only to tolerate but to welcome the differences...[47]

Adler's pattern of thinking is clear enough. The "infinite spiritual manifold," organicism, the interdependence of unique talents and specialties, and now the vocation of nations all speak in the same voice. Industrial society is the historic occasion when the "vocation of man" is advanced by the vocations of men.

Vocational Democracy

Adler was a spiritual democrat. All human beings were members of and participants in the ideal universe, the "spiritual manifold." But the ideal also has its reflections in experience. He must, therefore, deal with its political and economic outcomes. In his time, the historic "occasion" is the unique mission of the American republic. Peculiarly accessible to modernity, it invites reconstruction in the light of the new experience of human beings as democratic citizens and as workers in an industrial society. The key to a reconstructed politics is the idea of vocation.

> The theory of society which I have endeavored to indicate...may be labeled, "industrialism," or better "vocationalism"...It is a deplorable fact that owing to the spread of commercialism, the daily business of life...has come to be unconsecrated and unethicized...I agree with those who believe that the elevation of society can only come through the regeneration of the inner life...the intermediate motive of devotion to one's calling and through the medium of one's calling to society as a whole is sufficiently powerful and tangible to effect the desirable changes.[48]

Labor in an industrial society is a vehicle of identity. When asked what they are and do, people typically reply with a job title. Unless, however, we can move from work to vocation, an individuated identity and loyalty to others and to society generally will fail to appear. That is the disease of specialism; isolation dissolves society. But loyalty cannot be imposed. Rather, the conversion of occupation into vocation brings with it an experience of democratic society, an inclusive society of real individuals. It is, as it were, a natural outcome of the move toward the ideal.

Once again, the idealist is also the realist. People on the job demonstrate the importance of having the experiences that legitimate loyalties. "Bread and circuses" and even a bigger wage package will not do it. For us, today's efforts to redesign the workplace and the job reveal the fact. Thus, our business society works with the notions of the "team," of participation, of the diffusion of authority and the reduction of managerial hierarchy, indeed of the corporation as a moral and not just as a legal entity.[49] These notions all suggest the empirical soundness, albeit remarkably early in the industrial game, of Adler's insights and intuitions.

Failure to connect the ideal with commitment and with its symbols results in the *anomie* so evident in society and workplace alike. Cynicism becomes epidemic. In reaction, disillusioned "blue collar" workers become the twentieth century cadres of anti-democratic movements in politics and in religion. Loyalties cease to have a moral basis and become, instead, ways of acting out failure and frustration. In this context, already visible in the chauvinism, the anti-red scares, the bloody struggle against the unions, the racism and anti-Semitism of his own day, Adler searches for an alternative to irrational loyalties, blind loyalties. He is aware, too, of that other side of America, its history of finding moral scapegoats in the Irish, the Chinese, the middle-European immigrant. And in his experience as a German-American and of the "war spirit," he has fresh confirmation of a society that claims the dream but is unreconstructed. Moralism would not do. The alienation of work and worker opens the door to manipulation. Vocationalism is, therefore, a political necessity.

Vocation teaches the person the lessons of excellence and of mutuality. How then could these find political expression? Adler's suggestion is that an inter-vocational structure, already latent in the reconstruction of work, can also be a political structure. Politics can be "organized" too.

No doubt also motivated by events, Adler's vocational democracy is a response to the changing character of the American experience. An industrial society is not an agrarian society, not a rural society. Jefferson's America, "nation of honest farmers," is the description of a world that no longer exists. The people who inhabit the Republic are to be found clustered in larger and larger numbers in the modern city and at work in the modern factory. America has not only grown more populous, but its shape and its content are changing. Interests multiply and living styles are more varied than the founders of the Republic had dreamed possible.

Representative government becomes a puzzlement in idea and in practice. Citizenship itself is reduced to a merely "quantitative" device based on geography, an "aggregate" democracy as Adler puts it. Vote counting is not a sufficient method for achieving democracy and an "informed" electorate becomes problematic.

Although Adler is committed to the inclusive membership of all persons in the spiritual universe, he is not naive about the actual situation. People are in fact different as to their readiness and their capability, and this is not, could not be, reflected in mere head-counting. "One man, one vote" only sounds democratic. Elections, therefore, exhibit the error of confusing equality with identity. At the same time, Adler is suspicious of elites who are only usurpers of power. But mobs, in this instance the conforming Americans, the blind patriots of the warfare state, are the complement of elites. Although he lived before the rise of Fascism and Nazism, he knows that "masses" follow leaders and in turn that leaders need "masses" to achieve and maintain power. So it is that for Adler neither "status" nor "contract" would do as the basis for a democratic social order. Thus, his vision of the state as an "organized" democracy.

> The ethical aim of political reformation and reconstruction may be put in a single word, organization. The state and especially the democratic state must be organized. This means practically that the basis of representation shall be the vocational group...The lawmaking body on this basis will consist of representatives or delegates of the agricultural, the commercial, the industrial, the scientific group, *etc.* Women

belonging to these groups will exercise the franchise within them. There
will also be a distinct group of homemakers, motherhood will be
recognized as a vocation...[50]

Adler thus generalizes industrial competence beyond economic
processes and workplace activity.[51] Representation, and so policy-
making, is assigned to the vocational group. The meaning of the vote
changes. Indeed, Adler would say that the vote again has meaning.
To be sure, his thinking on this theme is sketchy. In the post-war
world of the 1920s, he seems in a hurry to set things down, aware of
his age and of his coming death. Thus, he misses the possibility that
there may well be other than vocational interests and that these too
might deserve a voice in the reconstructed state. Certainly the
settlement house experience had taught him and his colleagues that
ethnic and neighborhood loyalties are not only retrogressive and
certainly do not vanish. Constituencies that cross vocational lines may
have interests too. To take a current example, an interest in the
environment might suggest that citizen "naturalists" ought to have
representation as such. Adler, in other words, stretches the notion of
vocation out of shape and probably puts too much of a burden on it.
At the same time, given the abuse of "public opinion," the rise
of sloganeering and propaganda, of the kind of "yellow journalism"
that helped to produce the Spanish American War, Adler tries to
insure a sensible place for everyone as a member of the imagined
articulated and articulate public. An informed citizen was to be the
outcome of schooling and a free press. But the citizen is one thing in
a pastoral and rural culture, a culture of the "town meeting," and
quite another in the industrial city. In an unreconstructed industrial
society, too many people vote "early and often," and the political
"boss" controls the perquisites and the votes. Neither knowledge nor
power are broadly available. "Aggregate" democracy is not
democracy at all. For the political realists, that led to the conclusion
that the Enlightenment idea of democracy was simply outdated. As
Pareto put it,

> A political system in which the "people" expresses its "will" (supposing
> it to have one, which is arguable) without cliques, intrigues, lobbies and
> factions exists only as a pious wish of theorists. It is not observable in
> reality in the past or the present, either in the West or anywhere else...[52]

For Adler, realism led to reconstruction.
To be sure, there seems to be a resemblance between Adler's
vocationalism and European syndicalism. Certainly Adler's language

invites the comparison. However, such a comparison is superficial as the details quickly reveal. Syndicalism, after all, was a romantic and anti-intellectual movement that glorified violence, as in the general strike, and that aimed for the conquest of one class by another.[53] A more likely relative is "guild socialism." Charles Frankel describes it.

> The guild socialist movement...was at first largely a protest and an attempt to revive the medieval guild in reaction against the stale and uninteresting features of industrial production...The guild movement became more unmistakably socialist with the influence of S.G. Hobson who, in collaboration with A.R. Orage, wrote a number of books in which the prospects of the guild movement were made to depend upon the possibility of fostering labor control over industry...guild socialism...was also the specific medium for protecting democratic values against the centralization of industry whether capitalistically or socialistically organized...[54]

Certainly Adler was personally familiar with democratic socialism through his work with the International Ethical Union and with the Fabians who played an early role in the British Ethical Societies. Yet, he was careful to draw his own distinctions, whatever insights he may have gained from others. Once again, he is the idealist and his own person.

Discovering a Vocation

Reliance on education is a commonplace of liberal democratic thinking. The school is to be the method of politics and the widest and freest communication is the continuation of that method in adult life. The Constitutional guarantees of freedom of assembly and of the press are a pedagogical program. Adler, of course, draws upon American cultural and social history but again gives his own "spin" to it. Education as a politics also needs its reconstruction. Vocation, moreover, lends itself to the process for "every vocation on its ethical side is educational."[55] The new education, then, is to be industrial, *i. e.*, vocational. But it is not trade-school education at all, not a narrowly conceived training in skills and practices. As against this, skill is to be transformed by an ideal of service.

> Each vocation satisfies some one or more of the empirical human needs; but in the very act or process of doing so, it ought, in order to deserve the

name of vocation, to satisfy also a spiritual need, to contribute in a specific way toward the formation of a spiritual personality.[56]

Service in an industrial society is, of course, a creature of interdependence. It is, therefore the moral act of the unique individual who contributes to the emerging uniqueness of others. Service takes its meaning from the notion of irreplacability.

A reconstructed idea of citizenship is one implication of this political and educational reading of moral reciprocity. The citizen is competent because he or she is capable of the specialty. And that capacity is nurtured, is schooled. Citizenship education, therefore, is not a matter of civics lessons but of industrial and commercial activity. That is the source of political legitimacy.

Education properly conceived begins with the discovery of the individual's "leading interest." The universality and the differentiation of talent are therefore basic. The first task of the educator, of the parent as teacher as well as of the school itself, is to help the emerging personality find itself, to find that which will exhibit uniqueness in practice. So even the most intimate feature of the person, that which makes him or her exactly who he or she is, is an outcome of sociability, now the organized sociability of home and school. As Adler puts it, "The *caesura* in education will then fall about the sixteenth year. Before that, the task will be to lay the general foundations and to reconnoiter the individuality of the pupil..."[57]

The transformation of the schools to the end of the evocation of personality is the prerequisite of the transformation of political and of economic life. Education, then, is not only religious but political, or better, the religious life is inherently a political and economic life too. By contrast, the so-called trade school is as retrogressive as the "prep" school. Already visible at the turn of the century, Adler knew how quickly an invidious distinction among students was shaping American schooling. Already "tracking," although not yet called by that name, was assigning the many to meet the needs of the marketplace and the few to uppermiddle class privilege. Neither an industrial nor a democratic society could survive that kind of distinction.

Once again, Adler's ideas reflect the progressive movement in education. Dewey, typically, also calls for the integration of culture and labor in schooling.

While training for the profession of learning is regarded as the type of culture...that of a mechanic, a musician, a lawyer, a doctor, a farmer, a merchant, or a railroad manager is regarded as purely technical and professional. The result is that which we see about us everywhere, the division into "cultured" people and "workers"...While our educational leaders are talking of culture, the development of personality, etc...the great majority of those who pass under the tuition of the school regard it only as a narrowly practical tool with which to get bread and butter enough to eke out a restricted life...[58]

A trade emphasis has its consequences for the professional and the manager too, so privilege is not immune to the consequences of specialism. Indeed, all schools, even those using a classical or liberal arts rhetoric, are moving toward technicism, the substitution of training for education. Against this trend, the mere reassertion of classicism serves only to remind us of a dying civilization. Instead, vocation becomes a critical instrument in Adler's mind for the reconstruction of education, for the move toward its industrial future. "The ideal...is that the performance of a man may...correspond to the character which we ascribe to him as a moral being...the one thing to try for in education is to make every boy or girl capable...[to achieve] vocational excellence or perfection of work...[59]

Adler, typically, is the realist and not just the idealist in education too. "Reconnoitering the individuality of the pupil" requires careful and extended attentiveness to the growing child and the adolescent. Experience, as it were, is still prior to theory. As Adler put it, "difference is the ethical sign," but difference in experience must be found, not invented The attribution of worth and membership in the "spiritual universe" are forms that must be instantiated in the world we live in, in the school we teach and learn in. Indeed, when Adler dealt with schooling he had a genuine sense of the unpredictability of situations. Thus, "the school must become to a certain extent an experimental field for the purpose of ascertaining the kind of social service for which the pupils are best adapted..."[60]

Vocation, of course, is not a static idea for the individual or for industrial society. Experience evolves as the ethical personality acts intentionally and purposively. And society evolves as ethical personalities interact. This kaleidoscope image of the "having" of experience and of its outcomes means that the vocation develops too and is not merely a role description and set of skills that can be learned once and for all. Consequently, education has a continuing task as well. Indeed, Adler has a sense of development through lifestages which has import for vocation, for school, for reconstruction itself. He therefore remarks, "The ethical problems arising in the different vocations should be included in the programme for the education of adults."

Teachers have their special place in an organized society. They have their connections too and are not simply instrumental in helping others toward industrial citizenship. Practically, this means that

> [t]he teachers as an organized body, a vocational group, should also relate themselves to an organized body of parents. Home and school should not merely cooperate but interpenetrate. The interests and efforts of both are centered in the same young lives...Schools must be backed by the interest and appreciation of the community. Parents whose children are pupils of a school are for that particular school the best representatives of the community...[61]

Indeed, it is one of the ethical duties of the teacher to prevent letting the school fall into the trap of specialism.

Finally, schooling does not exhaust the work of education. For Adler, the lawyer, the judge, the statesman and the religious teacher are all members of the "educational" vocation. So while each has his or her skill and focus, there is always another and essential dimension to their vocations. In their vocational actions, they are always educating the community. Indeed, it is possible to interpret Adler's sense of the educational act of the vocationalist as a broad and even universal demand. The person engaged in business, in commerce, in agriculture and in craft also carries an educational obligation to peers and to the young. The themes of apprenticeship and mastery to which Adler turns in describing the development of character give content to that obligation. In a genuine sense, vocation is worth in action, and education is the process of the construction and reconstruction of worth.

Notes

[1] Among my present assignments is teaching business ethics in a university philosophy department. In the past decade or so, the number of texts has grown, as has interest in the subject. But, except for brief summaries of ethical "theory," usually at the beginning of a text or of a course, the treatment as such rarely deals with the reflexive interaction of situation and idea. Criticism of theory is still the subject matter of an "ethics" course but not of an applied ethics course.

[2] Bernard de Mandeville, *The Fable of the Bees*, London, 1732 (6th edition).

[3] It is worth noting that recent discussions of business ethics and the corporation sound very much like the Adler of the early twentieth century. The language is different, but the meaning is similar. For example, see

Robert Solomon, "Corporate Roles, Personal Virtues: An Aristotelian Approach to Business Ethics," *Business Ethics Quarterly*, Vol. 2, Issue 3, October 1993.

[4] In this regard, it is interesting to look at the "Introduction" and the "First Lecture" of the twelve he delivered at the Summer School of Ethics in Plymouth, Mass., 1894.

[5] William James, *The Moral Equivalent of War and Other Essays*, New York, Harper and Row, 1971.

[6] Adler, *The World Crisis*, pp. 34–35.

[7] Adler, *The World Crisis*, pp. 18–19.

[8] Felix Adler, "Spiritual Self Education," address, December 16, 1923, p. 16.

[9] Adler, *Reconstruction*, pp. 142–143; p. 155.

[10] Adam Smith, *The Wealth of Nations*, New York, Random House, 1937, pp. 734–735.

[11] Felix Adler, "Third Lecture," Plymouth, p. 34.

[12] Emile Durkheim, *The Division of Labor in Society* (1893), translated by George Simpson, New York, The Free Press, 1964, p. 228.

[13] After World War II and continuing the Durkheimian tradition, sociologists of labor worked on the social implications of the "division of labor" and its meaning. For a midcentury report, see Georges Friedmann, *Industrial Society*, edited by Harold L. Sheppard, New York, The Free Press, 1955. The management literature of the past decade or so is filled with reference to "team" work, productivity "circles," and similar images of the decentralization of authority. No doubt in part motivated by corporate and national interest, it is nevertheless the case that technical productivity is more and more likely to be organized these days to take account of the worker as person and not simply as "hand" or "eye." Indeed, a bestselling book, the fact itself a symptom, reported the trend. See Thomas J. Peters and Robert H. Waterman,Jr., *In Search of Excellence*, New York, Harper and Row, 1982.

[14] For a discussion of this theme, see James Rachels, *Created From Animals*, Oxford, England, Oxford University Press, 1991.

[15] For example, Nel Noddings, *Caring, A Feminine Approach to Ethics and Moral Education*, Berkeley, California, University of California Press, 1984.

[16] The classic statement of a labor theory of value is John Locke's:

every man has a property in his own person...The labor of his body and the work of his hands, we may say, are properly his. Whatsoever he removes out of the state that nature hath provided...he hath mixed his labor with and joined to it something that is his own...For this labor being the unquestionable property of the laborer, no man but he can have a right to what that is once joined to....*The*

Second Treatise of Government, New York, Hafner, 1947, p. 134.

[17] Even toward the end of his life, "this reform and that..." continued to trouble him. Adler, *Reconstruction*, p. 128.

[18] Erich Fromm, *Marx's Concept of Man*, New York, Ungar, 1966.

[19] Morton White, *Social Thought in America*, Boston, Beacon Press, 1957, p. 122. Citation is from E. R. A. Seligman, *An Economic Interpretation of History*, New York, 1902, pp. 112, 126.

[20] Once again, it is interesting to note how "future" history catches up with the Adler of the 1890s and the early twentieth century. For example, see Amartya Sen's essay, "Does Business Ethics Make Economic Sense?" *Business Ethics Quarterly*, Volume 3, Issue 1, January 1993.

[21] Friedman, *Industrial Society*, pp. 392–393.

[22] Adler, *An Ethical Philosophy*, p. 289.

[23] R. H. Tawney, *Religion and the Rise of Capitalism*, New York, Penguin Books, 1947, pp. 200–201.

[24] Adler, *The World Crisis*, pp. 192–193.

[25] For a discussion of professions see Adler, *An Ethical Philosophy*, Book IV.

[26] Durkheim, *The Division of Labor*, p. 40.

[27] Adler, "Fourth Lecture on Culture," p. 1

[28] Adler, "*An Ethical Philosophy*," pp. 261–262.

[29] Its interesting to compare Dewey with Adler on this point. As Lawrence Cremin writes,

Of all the dualisms Dewey attacked, none was more crucial to his view of progressivism than the ancient divorce between culture and vocation...For centuries, culture had meant the possession of certain kinds of knowledge marking the knower as a member of a superior social group...On two counts, then, that of exclusiveness and that of inequality, the historic view of culture was blatantly aristocratic...Dewey concluded...culture could embrace a much wider sphere of studies...including the sciences and trades if properly taught with the goal of growth in mind. *The Transformation of the Schools*, New York, Vintage Books, 1961, pp. 124–125.

[30] Felix Adler, "Matthew Arnold's Philosophy of Life," address, November 12, 1905, pp. 78.

[31] Adler, "Second Lecture on Culture," pp. 14–15.

[32] Morton White, *Social Thought in America*, pp. 2223. White's reference is to John Stuart Mill's *Essays on Some Unsettled Questions of Political Economy*, London, 1844, pp. 138–139.

[33] Adler, *Reconstruction*, p. 94.

[34] Adler, *An Ethical Philosophy*, p. 298.

[35] Adler, *The World Crisis*, p. 159.

[36] A typical comment sums up this view when Adler writes, "a similar motive

works in the competitive system and in socialism...Both are individualistic and naturalistic, though the latter is inclusive of all individuals" (*Reconstruction*, p. 125).

[37] Adler, *An Ethical Philosophy*, p. 290.

[38] Adler, *The World Crisis*, pp. 127–128.

[39] Adler, *Reconstruction*, pp. 94–95.

[40] Adler, *The World Crisis*, p. 196.

[41] Felix Adler, "The Foundation of a Better Social Order as Laid in Education," address, January 29, 1922, pp.1–3.

[42] Felix Adler, "The Ideal Culture for Businessmen," (1924) reprinted as a pamphlet by the American Ethical Union, New York, 1940, pp. 8–10.

[43] While Adler rejects the term "humanism," he is clearly announcing the kind of theme that Julian Huxley describes in *Religion Without Revelation*, New York, Mentor Books, 1958.

[44] Adler, "Third Lecture on Culture," pp. 3–5.

[45] John Dewey, *The School and Society*, in *Dewey on Education*, edited by Martin S. Dworkin, New York, Teachers College, 1959, pp. 42–43.

[46] Adler, *Reconstruction*, pp. 158–159.

[47] Adler, *The World Crisis*, pp. 24–25.

[48] Adler, "Tenth Lecture," Plymouth, pp. 2–3.

[49] One sign of a reinterpretation of the corporation today is what is called "stakeholder" theory. The corporation is a "community" with rights and duties assigned not just to owners and workers. Included as interested parties to be consulted are consumers, the environment, other corporations, the political and social communities in which the business finds itself, etc. For a typical discussion, see R.E. Freeman, *Strategic Management: A Stakeholder Approach*," Boston, Pitman, 1984. Under the inspiration of feminist moral theory, corporate life is also being reexamined under the rubric of an "ethics of care."

[50] Adler, *An Ethical Philosophy*, pp. 310–312.

[51] Adler's thought again has its kinship with Durkheim who wrote,

> Society, instead of remaining what it is today,...would become a vast system of national corporations. From various quarters it is asked that elective assemblies be formed by occupations and not by territorial divisions; and certainly, in this way, political assemblies would more exactly express the diversity of social interests and their relations. They would be a more faithful picture of social life in its entirety....Durkheim, *The Division of Labor*, p. 27.

[52] Vilfredo Pareto, *Sociological Writings*, edited by S.E. Finer, New York, Praeger, 1967, p. 270.

[53] For example, see Max Nomad, "The Evolution of Anarchism and

Syndicalism: A Critical View," in *European Ideologies,* edited by Feliks Gross, New York, Philosophical Library, 1948. Refer, also, to Georges Sorel's classic text, *Reflections on Violence.*

[54] Charles Frankel, "Social Views Since 1850," *Chapters in Western Civilization,* II, New York, Columbia University Press, 1948, pp. 214–215.

[55] Adler, *An Ethical Philosophy,* p. 289.

[56] Adler, *An Ethical Philosophy,* p. 293.

[57] Adler, *An Ethical Philosophy,* pp. 297–298.

[58] Dewey, *School and Society,* p. 39.

[59] Adler, "Tenth Lecture," Plymouth, pp. 10–12.

[60] Adler, "Tenth Lecture," Plymouth, p. 15.

[61] Adler, *An Ethical Philosophy,* p. 294.

IV

CULTURE AND CHARACTER

The Problem of the Self

The theme of reconstruction is heard again as Adler turns to the perennial religious question, "Who am I?" Adler has faced it before when he attributes worth to the human being. In a related way, he answers with a philosophy of work when he deals with the derivative question: what makes an ethical life possible in an industrial society? Now, a third question appears: what must be done by a self-conscious rational being like the human being in order to become more and more a creature of the ideal, a creature of worth and not of value? Adler's reply is a theory of religious education

As usual, Adler's starting point is a familiar notion, the idea of moral character.[1] To be sure, character has a decidedly conservative ring to it and so, in a sense, it is unexpected in Adler, the radical and the progressive, although not in Adler the Victorian gentleman. It brings with it, too, traditional associations with spiritual "election," inherited social status and, not least of all, moralism. When we hear it, we tend to think of the upright character, the virtuous character, the gentleman of character. Facing the brutality and opportunism of the industrial struggle to succeed, however, it also sounds not a little bit irrelevant. At the same time, therefore, character even becomes a semihumorous derogatory term, as in the village character, "he's a character" or cartoon characters. Today, of course, "character education" has been partly rehabilitated but with a decidedly conservative spin as the American faces rising crime rates, increasing numbers of singleparent families and social disarray.

Adler, as usual, works out his own meanings and approaches the theme as a way of solving the problem of self in an industrial society. Above all, he democratizes the notion of character. All human beings, and not just members of elites, can be characterful; *i. e.*, all human beings can achieve distinctive excellence in conduct and in lifestyle.

For Adler, character is to be the expression of the individuated biography, the moral personality. It is not the qualities that show up when a class or caste role is to be played. Performance is, of course, important. But a truly personal life cannot be a series of performances scripted by others or lived by general principles enunciated by others. By contrast, aristocratic society measures the person by the behavior considered proper to the class. In a related but surely less austere way, industrial society uses collective criteria too. In that society, character is reduced to the performance of designated tasks in accordance with non-personal mechanistic specifications. Rejecting both the aristocrat's *noblesse oblige* and industrial labor's job descriptions as appropriate moral models, Adler again tries for a "third way." A coherent pathway through life as it is lived is needed. Its name is character, and its outcome is identity. But the uniqueness of each person implies that character is not to be captured by generalized features. At best, these are forms and point a direction. To be an individual, however, is to instantiate the form in one's own way, to be a biographical "occasion."

Adler is searching for an ethical image of human beings, a moral psychology and a moral anthropology. Thereby, each of us would create examples for education that would motivate personal development and enable the human being to measure himself or herself by selfdetermined standards. But examples are not models and are not to be offered for imitation. What is the human being, then, is not a spectator's question. Its religious quality echoes Augustine's "What is man that Thou art mindful of him?" For Adler, independent of traditional theologies, this is translated into: What is a person that he or she should be mindful of himself or herself? And he might well add: What am I that I should be mindful of myself?

In search of character, Adler looks more deeply into the meanings of solitude, although he does not forget that the integrity of the self is always found in sociability. Unfortunately, the inner life has been encapsulated in the intimate experiences of birth, love, suffering, sadness and death. The quiet struggles of conscience point us inward too. But this move also isolates the intimate from the public. So, purpose-become-personal is yet another type of ethical experience to be reconstructed. In this context, worth as felt is the soul of tradition, the soul in action. Coming down from the "heaven beyond the heavens," the idea of the soul now points to the search for self consciousness in the world of human dispensability and mechanization.

Adler also looks around him, responding to the actual social situation. The "ties that bind" no longer bind. Already visible in his time, families, communities and loyalties are fragmenting in the industrial world of large numbers, increasing mobility and wage labor. Traditional values are at best problematic. Again, it is helpful to notice that Adler's reading of society is not peculiar to him. His voice is heard from within a neighborhood of liberal and radical social criticism. For example, John Dewey stated,

> The tragedy of the "lost individual" is due to the fact that while individuals are now caught up into a vast complex of associations, there is no harmonious and coherent reflection of the import of these connections into the imaginative and emotional outlook on life...The habit of opposing the corporate and collective to the individual...distracts attention from the crucial issue: how shall the individual refind himself in an unprecedentedly new social situation...[2]

Industrial experience confounds the question of personal identity. "Ragged individualism," as Dewey called it, is far from liberating and far from individuating. Competitiveness, rationalized as an innate drive for profit and success, is calculated to break the person apart, to fragment the soul. Never was the rhetoric of individual personality so prevalent and the reality so distant. The compulsive acquisition of things becomes a new kind of slavery. Emulation, "keeping up with the Joneses," becomes a guide to the personal life; society ennobles triviality. And, although troubled and dismayed, people cannot identify the sources of the problem because they believe, or are led to believe, that they are being made free by the market system. An economic game, a game of value, replaces a spiritual necessity. Sounding much like the Emerson of *The American Scholar,* Adler writes,

> The plan of cutting man into sections and then trying to see how these different sections would act if left to themselves, how the economic man would act, how the moral man would act, how the intellectual man would act, is a bad one....It treats man as if he were a worm and could be cut up into slices, each slice continuing to live a separate existence...[3]

Each of these separate existences, in turn, is in relationship to a sliced up part of society as well, business, religion, politics, the academy. Fragmentation is an irresistible and consistent pattern in the large and in the small. So it is that the family, the tribe, the state, all the forms of community that are natural to the human being are fragmented in turn, are reduced to mere utilities if they survive at all. Unlike social contract theorists, however, Adler does not conceive society merely as an instrument of self defense, an alliance of the weaker against the stronger. If, following Hobbes, human life is "brutish and short," the cause is not a "state of nature" but a failing society.

That, of course, is the empirical analysis that led thinkers like Durkheim to turn solidarity into a norm and that led most social theorists to reject the radical individualism of the anarchist. But, an empirical analysis cannot establish which road ought to be taken. There are many possible societies, many possible solidarities. Society can, therefore, exhibit both the vicious struggle for power that the "realists" describe and the loving cooperation of equals that the social democrat and the Christian describe. The issue for the person, the reconstructed soul, then, is to find out what kind of society meets the needs of the spirit and to set himself or herself the task of its achievement. Identity, typically for Adler, is simultaneously a social and a personal matter.

Industrial society is perfecting corporate organization and the phenomenon of "mass man." The individual, then, is a category and not unique at all. The modern city, soon to become the metropolis and in our time the megalopolis, makes it all the more difficult to find the person in the crowd. Adler's deliberate use of the term, "organization" is not intended just to highlight an extension of the biological notion of organism. Corporate and collective structures are and will be a fact of industrial life. They must be ethicized. And for the question of identity, the issue becomes figuring out how inwardness and social being in a corporate society are to be possible.

The modern city is a metaphor of the industrial process as a locus of the problem of identity. No longer are the wilderness and the desert accessible images although nostalgia and romance would turn to the American West and the South Sea Island in an admission of their absence. In the industrial city are found all of those productive capacities which are both the strength and the threat of industrial culture. But the new city has the additional capacity of anonymity. The individual is easily lost and as easily loses himself and herself.

> The population has gravitated to the city...the price of land rises, the slum appears...the family is too much squeezed for real family life...There must be room...Now...home life is not possible in a foul, filthy, reeking slum. So, they speak of the Housing Problem. I do not call it the Housing Problem. That suggests again something mechanical. It is the family problem...It is impossible to be an individual, a personality, always in the presence of others...solitude is indispensable to development...[4]

In the conditions of industrial society made manifest in the new city, the individual cannot find himself or herself. Instead, people become very competent to deal with the question, "What am I?" and they confuse that with the question of identity. In a revealing way, the typical answer is a job title, which in turn conveys a location in the hierarchy of economic status and function. Categories replace persons. So the theme of alienation is not simply social and political but spiritual, a matter of the soul. Specialism is but a social outcropping of this deeper difficulty. As Emerson put it, "The state of society is one in which the members have suffered amputation from the trunk and strut about so many walking monsters, a good finger, a neck, a stomach, an elbow but never a man."[5]

Adler, evidently more deeply influence by Emerson than he is prepared to admit,[6] knows that the person-become-thing is well on its way to becoming the rule of living. Marx, too, had put the same conclusion in his own fashion when he wrote,

> Money transforms the real human and natural powers into merely abstract ideas and hence imperfections, and on the other hand it transforms the real imperfections and imaginings, the powers which only exist in the imaginations of the individual into real powers...It transforms loyalty into vice, vice into virtue, the slave into the master, the master into the slave, ignorance into reason and reason into ignorance. He who can buy valor is valiant although he is cowardly...[7]

So Adler is in interesting company.

Character becomes a commodity to be bought and sold. It is a mark of a person's bank balance and not of his or her virtue. Thus, the "cash nexus" appears at the core of intimacy, corrupts the soul. This is not just the expression of a philosopher's sour temperament. There are facts enough to support the conclusion. Political office is bought and sold, and so the art of the *polis* becomes a commodity. "Honorary degrees" are often a reward for cash contribution and not a sign of learning. Possessions, and in particular the show of possessions, become the token of excellence.

To be sure, other societies and other cultures have not been innocent of reducing virtue to things and of granting privilege to property. It was, after all, the sale of indulgences that triggered the Reformation, and Jesus did throw the moneychangers out of the Temple, which means they were there in the first place. But industrial society universalizes the habit of marketability, the commercial spirit. It makes commerce general and pervasive, increases opportunities for the exploitation of others and the aggrandizement of the self. And, as it perfects the division of labor, it rationalizes the process to boot.

The search for a relevant inwardness, then, encounters new and massive obstacles. Nor can the search be postponed to another world, another time. For Adler, the move toward the ideal requires presence in the world as it is of the spiritualized, the ethicized, individual.

Absent the moral personality, and the future cannot make the move toward the ideal. Human beings and society alike will remain the victims of contingency. In such a condition, the human condition is not so much tragedy, where effort and failure combine to reveal excellence, but disaster.

> The problem of how to support and console the wretched multitudes of mankind in the interval that must elapse before the reform of conditions can take real effect; the problem of support and consolation in fatal sickness, on the deathbed, and in the harrowing recollection of irremediable and irrevocable wrongs done to others; the problem raised by the prospective extinction or the possible old age and degeneration before the extinction of mankind...all these problems should be taken together...From one peg they all hang, on one cardinal idea they all depend...the idea of personality as positively defined...The ascription of worth to man...is the fundamental problem of all...[8]

Reconstructing personality using the ideas of worth and of vocation takes on an emotional dimension. They are not simply offered as concept and practice and critique. Now, they are to become *my* problem. I am no longer outside of the subject. I am implicated in it.

We are in the presence, then, of "ultimate concern," to use Paul Tillich's phrase for the shaping ideal of the religious life. That presence and its evolution are what turns education under the inspiration of the ideal into religious education. As Alfred North Whitehead put it,

> The essence of education is that it be religious...A religious education is an education which inculcates duty and reverence. Duty arises from our potential control over the course of events. Where attainable knowledge could have changed the issue, ignorance has the guilt of vice. And the foundation of reverence is this perception, that the present holds within itself the complete sum of existence, backward and forwards, that whole amplitude of time which is eternity.[9]

For Adler, still the Kantian, duty is the unconditioned ought, although my particular duties emerge from my personality, my relationships and my moment in time, and not from universal law. Reverence appears as the moral activity of "eliciting" the unique potency of the other and thereby shaping one's own moral development. The context is a sense of history. For the reconstructed soul, all of these now become autobiographical.

The Capacity for the Infinite

The idea of worth is Adler's restatement of Kant's "end-in-itself." But for Adler, the idea is a social, temporal and personal matter all at once. Its historic occasion is the American Republic and its eighteenth century ancestry. Obviously, the idea of worth is a non-theological and non-traditional reading of the Christian soul. It is that feature of the being of the human being that tells us he or she cannot legitimately be sacrificed or invaded. It is thus an ethical reconstruction and a requirement of human relationships, not an eternal substance to be saved or damned. The idea of the soul has to be rescued not just from an outdated theology and the event of "mass" experience but also from the erosions of Enlightenment secularism and atomism. Adler's agenda is full and complicated.

Looking inward as the contemplative does will not satisfy Adler's project. Introspection implies that all alone and by oneself it is possible to arrive at meaning and personality. Introspection's metaphoric location is the desert. But, for Adler, intimacy is a social matter. So as I search out myself as an object of my imagination, I am always aware of my self-in-relation. But what is it that I am aware of? G. H. Mead, another participant in the progressive neighborhood, is most helpful in describing this self-consciousness.

> Recognizing that the self cannot appear in consciousness as an "I," that it is always an object, *i. e.* a "me,"...what is involved in the self being an object? ...a "me" is inconceivable without an "I." And to this reply must be made that such an "I" is a presupposition but never a presentation of conscious experience, for the moment it is presented it has passed into the objective case...an "I" discloses itself only by ceasing to be the subject for whom the object "me" exists...But the subject attitude which we instinctively take can be presented only as something experienced...[10]

Industrial society, then, can hide but it cannot succeed in destroying the person. So, instead, it exploits the soul. It assimilates identity with the commercial "personality," the externalization and approval of the signs of social success. A "winning" personality, a "pleasing" personality and the like are the creations of a commercial mentality. In fact, this transformation is another way of hiding, a suppression of self, and this is a source of industrial malaise. We know and yet are tempted to deny that personality, at its core, is out of reach. It cannot be manipulated or suppressed without paying the price of self denial. But even the denial forces self consciousness upon us. The situation is ultimately intolerable.

Following Mead's thought, when the self is brought to consciousness, even to self-consciousness, it ceases to be what it is and becomes other. Now, under a commercial inspiration, this other becomes a technique for suppression. As the existentialists were to put it, I am emptied of my self. The effort to ethicize the soul, to make it inviolable in principle by attributing worth and membership in the spiritual manifold to it has then not only a pragmatic intention but a psychological ground.

This ineffable "I" is indeed an elusive subject, but it is no less real for all that. It is not merely subjective in the sense of mere taste, mere feeling, *etc.* By nature, it cannot be put out there for examination, so efforts to talk directly about it must fail. It is had and acknowledged, but it can only be pointed to by metaphor, by poetry. We know it in personal experience but have trouble doing more than confess its presence. Adler's appeal, then, is ultimately to a *felt* individuality.

Adler, although he sometimes called himself a "mystic," is troubled by the idea that anything could be ineffable, *i. e.,* excluded from the discourse of inquiry, in this instance ethical inquiry. He is, to that extent, still the Enlightenment figure, the student for whom knowledge is a moral priority. To be sure, he speaks on occasion of the "unfathomable depths of personality," but he is uncomfortable when he does so. Ethical experience, after all, is supposed to lead to a "science of ethics." But the intimacy of mysticism forces Adler to admit that personal experience is ultimately unavailable to shared experience. He does not try to evade the fact that the individual as subject can only be aware of his or her own inner life and can only by extension, by an act of moral imagination, attribute a like awareness to others. The process of attributing to the human being what cannot be found by observation, the process which appears in his discussion of worth, is as process learned from the necessities of experience itself. It is, at the same time, an imperfect method for talking about that which cannot be talked about. Attributing worth and the like may seem to use the language of the axiom but the process is finally metaphoric.

William James describes Adler's situation accurately when he identifies the "marks" of mystical experience.

I. Ineffability. The handiest of the marks by which I classify a state of mind as mystical is negative. The subject of it immediately says that it defies expression...

II. Noetic quality. Although so similar to states of feeling, mystical states seem to those who experience them to be also states of knowledge...[11]

Stephen Wise, Rabbi of New York's Free Synagogue and a fellow religious and social reformer, rightly identifies this feature of Adler's thought and practice when he says, "Though he spelt the name of God other than we do, he was a great religionist. Adler was one of the truest of modern mystics."[12] And although uncomfortable, Adler did not hesitate to draw the moral implications of intimacy, the privacy of the inner life. Even here, however, reciprocity and sociability are at work. Intimacy teaches the lesson of a respect for boundaries, for the integrity of self and other. Inviolability is not simply an ethical imperative for social relationships and, in particular, industrial social relationships. It is in the first instance a fact of the spirit. Adler's attitude toward psychoanalysis is symptomatic.

[H]e (Adler) was opposed to any kind of scrutiny of the intimate private life which psychiatry and especially psychoanalysis was promulgating...My mother was one of the members of the group studying child nature...This group began to go roaring ahead and, of course, uncovered Freud...[They] got to the point of intensive exploration which offended Dr. Adler...he felt that there was something inviolate about the core of the human spirit which should not be probed....[13]

Adler is surely aware of Freud and the Freudianism of the early twentieth century, although he makes no direct references to either in his addresses or his writings. In his judgment, they loosen the bonds of the moral imperative and cast doubt on the possibility of universal moral law. Psychology, going where it has no business to be, is then one more instance of the dangers of naturalism, the dangers inherent in lacking a *telos,* an ideal. Of course, therapy's aim is the achievement of insight. But at the same time it denies the appropriateness of taking an ethical point of view. Such a view is said to be Victorian, oppressive and, worst of all, out-dated. The objectivity claims of the sciences are carried over into the fields of intimacy.[14] The outcome is to make moral anarchy, amoralism and sensuality legitimate. Conscience and guilt are transformed into symptoms. So, as Phillip Rieff puts it in his critique of a so-called neutral therapy, "The good life is entirely a matter of living up to the promise of the senses, so far as the special limits of a given culture will allow."[15]

Of course Adler's radical isolation of intimacy from inquiry presumes a mechanistic model of the universe and still builds on the Kantian distinction between the *noumenal* and the *phenomenal.* A more subtle and biological world image suggests the possibility of a less rigid and less de-personalized view of objectivity. I think, for example, of Dewey's notion of "inter-subjectivity" and of recent work in the philosophy of science.[16] On the other hand, the manipulations of the mass media, of "human engineering" and of interest-group politics suggest that Adler's caution is not simply to be dismissed.

Adler's views of the inner life benefit from a reconstructed notion of the sacred which is, like the soul, democratized and humanized. Yet, he is realist enough to recognize that the uniqueness of the human being can be simultaneously claimed and denied. Worth and value are always in dialectical relationship to each other. Inviolability, then, is a defense against the erosions of the rule of value. It directs attention as well to how we are to treat the "wretched" now, and not merely in some ideal future. Typically, Adler remarks,

> the notion of end being bound up with the notion of organism exists in idea only and not in fact...it cannot serve us in the business of explaining nature at all but only of evaluating it...The organic idea...is a directive to conduct...We are to regard each human being not as if he were already an end*perse* but in such a way as to help him to become a *telos*, a true member of an organic system, that is to say a personality and therefore indispensable in his place.[17]

As usual, Adler is aware of how easily this appeal to the ideal can be interpreted as "mere moralism." So, again, he turns to ethical experience in order to point out the realism of his way of seeing the human being. With Mead, he recognizes and expects us to recognize that when we act, "there is another 'me' criticizing, approving, and suggesting and consciously planning, *i. e.,* the reflective self."[18] Further reflection, Adler says, shows a "desire for distinctiveness." Informal observation as well as more disciplined inquiry reveal the presence of that desire in nearly everyone. We seek to dress differently, cook differently, speak differently. For all that we have a common biology and a shared history, we search for personal styles that range from the most superficial to the most significant, from the most underplayed to the most outrageous. We cherish our own special memories, share them privately with those who are invited to enter our lifeworlds. Above all, as Adler puts it, we want very much for our lives to have "some value, some significance...in our own eyes."[19] Even choosing to be anonymous, hiding in the crowd like Kierkegaard's "hidden Christian," in reaction to the pressures of conformity and style, exhibits the desire for significance.

Against this desire for distinctiveness as a personality is a market society. It does not, as such, try to suppress the desire so much as to transform it, to use it for its own purposes and to manipulate it. The superficialities are its strategy. Distinctiveness is thus reduced to possessions, and possessions are reduced to mass-produced and indistinguishable consumer goods. For Adler, it is not sensible, however, simply to condemn "materialism," as the pulpit is likely to do. Instead, the corruption of distinctiveness by commercialism is a motive for reconstruction.

> The common saying is that man has a soul. I should like to amend this by saying that we come into the world with the possibility of a soul and that the aim of life is to convert this into an actuality...to become a...personality, to acquire distinctive selfhood. The work we do...is a means of developing [it]...the occasion of coming in touch with reality and of importing the solidity of reality into [our] inner world....In the workshop, the soul is born....[20]

The vocation is, then, a religious idea seen from another side, as it were, the side of the nurtured and nurturing soul. The vocation is to combat the consumerist norms of industrial culture; so it is the locus and means of intimacy as well as of social and political reconstruction. The specialty appears as a personal act and not simply as a skill or art. It is practiced by a named being. My product carries my signature. Self-consciousness and inviolability, the soul in short, are to be facts of the reformed workplace as much as of material productivity.

Distinctiveness means to be recognized as who I am and not simply as what I do. In the first instance, that is a task of self-awareness and self-consciousness. But for Adler the self is the social self, so awareness and consciousness are transactional too. The industrial setting is both an opportunity for the widest distribution of transactions and at the same time a deterioration of all transactions. As an opportunity, Adler writes, "what is (popular) culture? Culture is the desire to rise above the commonplace...that is at least a beginning..."[21] Unfortunately, however, the rule of efficiency leads us to take "short cuts" to distinction. Nor is this only a workplace and marketplace phenomenon. Adler speaks, for example, of the "religious pose," the effort to establish in another's eyes that one is a "friend of God." In the anxiety for short cuts there is a certain pathos. For ultimately, appearance without reality cannot help but fail. The false distinctiveness of a "cultured" elite, of a "religious" *poseur* and the like, is driven by the needs of the collectivity. The role does not emerge from the individual as such, from the soul as such, and so does not serve to nurture personality. It is but another externality. As Adler puts it, the world becomes a stage in which we are "playing someone else."[22]

In a sense, Adler's analysis of role-playing can also be understood as a commentary on the inappropriate presence in the adult of a developmental stage suitable to the child. One might say that industrial society infantalizes the person. Adler the schoolman surely appreciates the role of drama and play in the life of the child and the adolescent. To enlarge the educational experience is to play the other's part as if it were one's own. From the process reflection grows. Further, Adler understands the moral value of what G. H. Mead calls the "generalized other." Being able "to see ourselves as others see us" is part of growing up and part of keeping morally awake. But Adler fails to address the business of "playing someone else" in a more complete way because of his anxiety about industrial society. The innocence and educational value even for the adult of "dressing up," of acting the part, of entering another's character, even a fictional character, are left out of his discussion.

Adler's overwhelming concern for the dangers of industrialism to individuality and the ideal personality in a sense betrays him. It is, after all, good to "get out of one's self" in order to gain perspective on one's self and appreciation of the other. The social self is also a society in itself, the presence not just of a "me" but of many "me's" in me. Memory and history people the self too. But the role-playing demands of industrial culture in effect commercialize the "generalized other." These roles, sadly, are not the nurturing, teaching and joyous experiences of humanity's natural urge for the dramatic and the comic. And this, for Adler, is the point that cannot be missed.

Of course, as in all things, human beings must fail in their search for distinctiveness, in trying to be an "original and not a counterfeit." Yet, the search goes on even against industrial society. The soul, for the Christian, is a matter between the communicant and his or her God. For Adler it is to be found "between man and man," as Martin Buber puts it. So the deteriorated roles of modern society serve also as an ethical experience calling for reconstruction. For all their superficiality and lack of individuality, the roles we are expected to play are latent with moral possibilities. Not least of all, people now have access to a plethora of roles. Once upon a time, they would have been condemned if they dared to assume a role that was not theirs. "A cat may look at a king," but woe to him who tries to play the king. The notion of the malleability of the human being which a fluidity of roles dramatizes is also an opportunity of modern culture. As Adler argues,

> The fault of even the best...systems (Stoicism, Pythagorianism, Christianity, etc.)...is that they all think of the self as if it were a kind of statue to be chiseled with a superfluity taken off here and a deeper line to be engraved there...whereas we think of the self as a power....an instrument of progress...instead of the scraping idea of self...of removing stains or excesses....[23]

Thus, in dramatic form, the soul is an outcome, a continuing outcome between being and becoming.

But if "man does not yet have a soul" as Adler writes, what is it that is in process and what is it that has an identity? That is, at least discursively, a mystery. Of course, he knows that identity is always in the present. Yet it changes, matures perhaps, and still remains the "same." Language, at least a language of nouns, verbs and modifiers, unfortunately freezes the process and forces the mistakes of a false identity upon us. We look for denotations like the "immortal soul," the "human spirit," "human nature" and the like. And denotations seem to fix things in place and in time. This is Adler's critique of "static" views of the soul. They ignore development.

When we turn to our experience, however, identity is not all that obscure and its development not all that mysterious. William James, also trying for a dynamic and biological view of self, catches experience when he writes,

> When Paul and Peter wake up in the same bed, and recognize that they have been asleep, each one of them mentally reaches back and makes connection with but one of two streams of thought which were broken by the sleeping hours...so Peter's present instantly finds out Peter's past and never by mistake knits itself onto that of Paul's...He *remembers* his own states while he only *conceives* Paul's...[24]

The power of the developing self is realized in the interaction with other selves. Adler thus carries over the assumption that the human being is a social being into his discussion of the soul. If sociability and transaction are self evident, however, the question of how they will appear in industrial society continues to be troubling. So the move is made from ontology to ethics.

> The individual is to become a person through his relations to the various
> groups to which he successively belongs...the family...the
> vocation...the state...the international society....The rule of
> development in these relations is the rule of action and reaction...always
> taken jointly. The right effects are those that stimulate the most vitally
> the nature of others and which in their reflex evoke the most vital faculty
> in the self....[25]

Of course, even the best of us falls short of originality. Neither distinctiveness nor inviolability are ever actually achieved. In any society there are extrinsic pressures that shape us and our roles. That, in part at least, is what it means to be in a society. Read as fate and inheritance, for example, that is how human beings have traditionally interpreted their status and station in life. Industrial society, by bringing this process down to earth and making it transparent, so to speak, makes the fact more visible and so accessible to reform. In an industrial society, complaints about mobility and rootlessness are typical. But these have another side. So again, the evil of industrialism is also its good.

Because failure is inevitable and frustration its consequence, it is not enough to deal only with the actual situation, not enough to be only a reformer. A certain attitude and perspective, a sense of the inadequacy of our efforts in the world, must also shape the approach to self and other.

> [I]f we are to preserve a man's respect for himself as a moral being, we
> must find a ground on which he can maintain his self esteem apart from
> the material conditions in which he is placed...The betterment of social
> conditions is sure to be gradual. The slum ought to be abolished
> immediately but until it goes we must find a reason to respect the man in
> the slums even now, and a reason why he should respect himself even
> now...[26]

Worth, then, carries the burden of identity too. In the world of being and doing and getting, the world most clearly instantiated by industrial society, "countless multitudes exist who go and come without leaving behind them an appreciable trace of their existence...On the grounds of value, I fail to see how...the sacred rights of every human being, the basis of our ethics and...of our democracy can be maintained...."[27]

Yet, rights and therefore respect are spiritual essentials and not simply contractual agreements. Constitutional provisions are only as strong as politics allows them to be. Worth is not subject to the ballot, however, and so serves as the formal basis of a notion of human rights. But where in ethical experience can a ground for rights be found? Adler, continuing his development of a philosophic psychology, locates that ground in the feeling of resentment.

> The circle is to be drawn so as to comprise all those who show or are capable of showing resentment against an injury done to them not as a harm but as a wrong. For this kind of resentment which we meet with even among primitive peoples is a sign of the operation in them...of the idea that they are the possessors of a nature deserving of respect on its own account, of a nature that possesses worth....[28]

To be sure, Adler is not foolish enough to claim that because a person feels resentment at harm, he or she will necessarily extend protection against it to others. But from the experience of resentment it is possible to move toward a more objective and inclusive notion of rights. As he put it, "What I grant to myself as a rational being must be granted to all other rational beings." The direction of reconstruction is clear. Its source in experience is also clear. I may violate your rights, but as a rational being I am in a position to know that I am doing so. It is a commonplace of the family and of the classroom, for example, that accusations of unfairness are understood at a very early age. Recent research by psychologists like Lawrence Kohlberg and his students into moral psychology verifies the trans-cultural presence of that sense of the fair and the unfair The legal theorist, Edmond Cahn, makes a similar point when he writes of a "sense of injustice."[29]

Adler's mysticism, his sense of the ineffability of the inner life, is not, then, left only to the inner life. Conduct as well as identity is its outcome. Indeed conduct, reflecting inward so to speak, shapes the inner life and so builds or destroys identity. The marketplace and not the monastery remain Adler's home. Only in that way can mysticism avoid being an excuse for "mystification" and moral irresponsibility.[30]

Adler is very much the intuitionist. But this, by itself can all too easily lead to moral anarchy. So intuition must be corroborated by conduct. Nor is self knowledge an end in itself. Identity makes a difference not just to the self but to other selves and to the world. It is not locked away to be appreciated, Midas-like, in the strong-room of the self. As Adler puts it,

Self knowledge...is the supreme aim. But self knowledge...for the sake of
the illumination it casts on the world...self knowledge whereby to
overcome the sense of alienness that so deeply troubles us...[self
knowledge] as a means of making our peace with the universe...to
see...fellow human beings despite their repulsive traits...as potential
spiritual companions....[31]

The mind of the human being, Adler notes is "architectural."
So unlike other beings, identity can make sense of its inward, outward
and active features. Thus, we need not be paralyzed by the images
Adler puts forth in such abundance. Identity is the "power" to act
toward an ideal future. It is the "datum" of my experience of myself
in the present. It is social in both its development and connections. It
is the location of my feelings of violation and of resentment. It is the
center of motivation. And yet, it is "I."

With identity and self as the keys to an ethical philosophy of
living, Adler has worked out an anthropological and psychological
content to the attribution of worth and to membership in the spiritual
universe. By locating moral achievement in the achievement of
selfhood, of personality, he minimizes the moral dangers of failure.
Thus, when in the world ethical conduct fails to elicit equivalent
response from another, as it surely does on occasion, the temptation to
cynicism grows. Yet, when I know that my experience is like yours,
no matter what your conduct may be, I am not without recourse. I
know that you desire distinctiveness, feel resentment, know what it is to
be morally harmed. I therefore have reason not to surrender the
human connection by treating you as simply evil and as simply alien.
I have grounds for reaching out and across. In this way, in the
relationship of soul to soul, the spiritual manifold serves as a blueprint
for the architectural mind of the human being. I can be realistic and
ethical at the same time. I need not deny misery and brutishness, but I
need not surrender to them either.

The Possibility of Personality

To dwell in inwardness is the mistake of the otherworldliness of
traditional religion where the relationship is between soul and God.
Typically, the soul is alone and passive. The language is one of
opening up to, emptying oneself, obedience. Damnation is, in many
traditions, a separation from God. For Adler, the vocation of the soul,
however, is to be found in reworking oneself. But this is an active
relationship, a transaction of soul and soul which shows up in the

actual and finite world of ordinary experience. The finite is instrumental for the infinite.

Adler does not entirely escape dualism since he does distinguish the ideal and the real. Yet, while distinct, they are not separated realms of being. The ideal is potent for the actual; the actual is the stimulus of the ideal. The soul finds its work in experience but its outcome in the ideal.

> The ethical aim is the development of personality...[which] is to be distinguished from individuality...a fundamental difference between value and worth....To ascribe worth to men is to ascribe to them an ideal character in no wise justified by their actual behavior....The idea of worth....sees [man as] a being essentially active, whose very life consists in affecting the life of others...[32]

The "city of man" is not the realm of the devil. Nor does Adler dissect our presence in the world into isolated and disconnected presences. We live and act in a world that gives the illusion that there is a sharp split between work and leisure, public and private, economics and politics or soul and substance. But, in fact, we carry our memories, habits, temperament wherever we go and are. We are organisms with memories. So Adler is, for all his use of oppositional categories, seeking ways of overcoming dualism without surrendering the analytic truths it contains.

The soul is potent and active in the world. So the natural question is: potency for what and with whom? The reply, as we have already seen in other contexts, is potent for self development, the achievement of distinctive personality. But at the same time, becoming oneself requires the actions of others.

It is not possible, however, to deduce in some *a priori* way the existence of other rational beings from the existence of any one of them, *i. e.,* from my own existence. The Cartesian possibility is not available. But experience does present us with unavoidable others. Some of them, at least, seem to be rational beings like ourselves. They too claim distinctiveness and resent being wronged. From this and from the knowledge of my own selfhood, a picture of the social self emerges. But it is not so much witnessed as felt. My identity thus has a public dimension. With this move, the notion of the human being as a social animal is transformed into the ethical and political notion of the "public." Of course, this is particularly apt if reconstruction is to take a democratic direction.

As such, the social relationship is ethically indeterminate. All kinds of relationships exist or are possible. An ethical relationship, on the other hand, is based on the recognition that,

> it is of prime importance to bear in mind that the public and the private nature are both embraced within the same human personality...my life is intertwined with that of others....So far therefore as I am in social relationships...I cannot act independently....I am not purely self determined...[33]

Adler's continuing concern in exploring personality is to emphasize its social nature. Thus, the "false individualism" of *laissez-faire* economics must be exposed and rejected along with other atomistic views of personality. The mystic strain in Adler finds identity in inviolability. But at once, that is inherently a social idea, *i. e.*, to have meaning inviolability presumes some other who may violate me and who ought to respect me. The social critic must make the effort to free that self from its temptation to hiddenness. Ethical experience thus demonstrates sociability, and reconstruction needs it. So, the person must distinguish that which he or she alone can know of himself or herself, the "I" that can only be felt by me, and that which is accessible to relationships, the "I" as a center for reaching toward other "I's." The self does not simply melt away into society. Neither self nor society are absolute terms. And just as the self is at least an "I" and a "me," so society is pluralized as well.

> I have tried to show that the social relations are spheres of personality (which) cannot be separated by hard and fast lines...a father, for instance cannot act within his own sphere without affecting the well being of the mother and of the children. The lines of influence pass to and fro in endless ways from sphere to sphere...that is what is meant by an organic relationship....[34]

Since the self is a social self, it is clear enough that the soul is affected by others, individually and collectively. The soul ought to be inviolable, but there is no guarantee that it will be It is in fact not untouchable. It is subject to influences and exerts influences. Unlike the Stoic or the Christian soul, Adler's soul cannot retreat into itself for safety. But, once having granted that transactional fact of experience, we have also opened the door to the crippled self, the self that is both harmed and that can do harm to others. In fact, that is precisely what describes the ethical problematics of industrial society. The task, then, is to rebuild society as a network of morally effective relationships for the sake of the soul. Social action, if you will, is an essential and perpetual implication of having a soul, of being religious.

Rebuilding society, however, is not simply the negative act of destroying the things that cripple the soul, important as that may be. The duties of respect for the worth of the person and the recognition of inviolability in others are typically negative. They deliver the message, "hands off." Adler surely sees the need for prohibitions and limits. But ethical experience has its affirmative requirements too. Ethics is not simply a list of "thou shalt nots." Adler, then, does not take the Kantian pathway of distinguishing categorically prescribed duties which are obligatory and gratuitous moral acts which are discretionary. Instead,

> the point...is that organization means moralization, that the various groups into which we successively enter are for us so many stages of a progressive moral education....The organic groups into which we successively pass become increasingly comprehensive and inclusive...in learning to treat these manifold and diverse interests as if they were our own interests our social self is developed....[35]

Although Adler talks about stages, they are neither the developmental moments of recent psychological theory nor are they ritualized dramatizations of spiritual progress. Adler's interest is in ethical development, and it is for that reason that he divides biography into six stages.[36] First, there is infancy and childhood. Adler's characterizes the moral status of the child as "right subjection." At this stage, unequal relationships of authority are legitimate. But this authority has its ethical justification, its objective reasons, and is not simply the power of the strong over the weak. In this relationship, the adult's burden is particularly heavy since the transaction is most demanding on the adult. The child, while active, is primarily a recipient. The adult is to be an example to the child of how to live by self-chosen rules, since it is precisely because the adult is defined as someone with a moral personality that he or she can serve as an example. Demanding obedience as such will not do. Mere conformity to external rules, which is so typical of adult and child relationships, is moral failure and in fact makes authority immoral. Putting this another way, the appeal to conformity reveals that the adult is not really a moral adult and so has no right to authority at all.

A parent's advice to the child, therefore, is "do what is right" and not "do what is socially expected." Of course, these may coincide, but they may also conflict. Integrity, then, is not reserved to adulthood but appears as a developing moral dimension of experience at the earliest stage of life. Obviously, Adler is not addressing himself to the more sophisticated and abstract uses of integrity. But he is thinking of the ways that children establish loyalties to each other and to their families, exhibit a sense of fairness, accept the legitimacy of sensible rules and the like. Moreover, as the child develops, he or she learns that the authority is not the adult's as such but the moral ground from which the adult speaks. Thus, the parent's added message is, "do what is right" not because I ask or tell you to but because it is the right thing to do. So status and position are not as such moral justifications. Again, experience suggests that this is not beyond the capacity of the childhood. Thus, the bully, the sneak, the liar are typical classroom characters and are typically suspect by most if not all students. Where the moral demand is beyond the capacity of the child, inappropriate to his or her stage, it may be offered as a moral demand, but it really is not. It is, instead, a prudential rule and only that. To do what is right, for Adler, is always personal and unique. Conduct is not its expression except as an outcome of emerging identity. I feel the moral demand in my own way although it sounds like the same moral demand. The example set before the child is complicated but not unrealistic.

From childhood, we move to adolescence. Here subjection is challenged and relationships are reinterpreted in the light of evolving moral capacities.

> The relation between the adolescent boy and girl and the parents...as illustrating in a way that young persons can understand the general conception of the ethical relation as *reciprocal*. The youth should be shown that he cannot only be a recipient of benefits, that he can be a real help...chiefly by sympathetically entering into the problems and difficulties with which they contend....At the same time, the young son or daughter will...gain an invaluable preparation for comprehending the difficulties under which the effort to live must be carried on.[37]

The teenager searches for independence. The danger is at both extremes, that it will be premature or that it will be delayed. Later adolescence is also a time for serious "prevocational" exploration. Adolescence, then, is from Adler's point of view a moment where subtle judgment and likely failure are present. Hence his concern with the high school as a strategic institution.

By early middle life, the vocation has been identified. The individual's talent has begun to express itself in "social service." A threefold relationship typifies this stage of ethical development.

Using a vocational imagery but remembering that vocational performance is also an educational act, this is the time for relationships to masters, to coworkers and to apprentices. The exercise of skill and knowledge shapes personality. In later middle life, vocations mature so as to "quicken the vocational activity in all related callings." The personality is ready to be a significant moral influence in the development of selves. Vocational mastery is on the horizon.

Old age is a time for summing up. Relationships have been well learned. The capacity for coherent reflection and so for transmission to next generations has been refined. In a striking phrase, Adler speaks of old age as a time for "right abdication." The mood is one of satisfaction with achieved mastery. At the same time, the aged personality extends a "welcome" to the other. Finally, facing death, the time arrives for "right farewell."

From Adler's point of view, the most powerful biographical position is not that of mastery but of surrender. Right abdication is a joyful and willing act. Until that is possible for us, mastery holds us in subjection. We have not masterful enough to let go, to make room. Or, putting this another way, we are not yet distinctive enough as personalities to be able to yield without resentment. An ethical surrender is not forced upon us by our successors but freely chosen and so secure. For a spiritual being, freedom is the final term. Its empirical sign in the workplace, in the family and in the community is the felt rightness of the abdication.

> The simile under which life is represented as a hill with an upward incline and thereafter a downward slope may be true of man physically and even intellectuality. But it is not true of him spiritually. It need not be. The highest point may be reached at the very end.[38]

The soul is prepared for its completion. It is not surprising that this last stage of Adler's typology echoes Buddhist thought. Adler had from the earliest days been an appreciative student of Eastern religions, as of mysticism. Without directly acknowledging these sources, he is nevertheless attempting the reconstruction of salvation from an otherworldly judgment to a this-worldly process. In the imagery of moral stages, this reconstruction acquires, as it were, a certain dramatic unity. When we are able to surrender freely and without resentment, we have "saved our souls alive," as Adler puts it.

Adler, in short, has sketched a normative biography. Continuous reintegration of the self, of how it experiences itself, is the mark of moral maturity. Arrival and departure and all that happens in between are the locus of the soul's development. Stages provide Adler with moments of judgment but, not least of all, with guides to the design of institutions like schools, continuing education and vocational reconstructions. The "pains of existence," the frustration to which Adler returns over and over again and which appear in their special way at each stage, are finally resolved in "right" dying.

The Three Shadows

An ethical biography is not an actual biography. Childhood may become permanent, as for instance when brain damage prevents development. Mastery may never be attained since the job may indeed become a dead end. And death will likely be an interruption and not a completion. Thus, the road between value and worth is never traveled without spiritual pain, the pain of always falling short of the ideal. The norm, then, may be spiritual freedom, but it is never entire. Human life is inevitably inadequate to the ideal. In a sense, we hear in Adler's normative biography the story of Moses. The promised land is visible but it will not be entered. The river will never be crossed.

Each stage along the way has its characteristic moral difficulties. The adult may fail to be morally objective when facing the child's need for rightful subjection. The freedoms of adolescence may be prematurely taken or mistakenly delayed. Irreverence towards colleagues and resistance to abdication are not surprising. Although each stage is the occasion of its particular failure, existence as such has its spiritual pains, its existential pains, too. Thus it is that Adler addresses the "three shadows," suffering, sorrow and sin. These appear at each stage in a special way. But, with these he also gives voice to his sense of the tragic quality of human life as such. In this way, too, he takes account of evil without trapping himself into an insoluble "problem of evil."

Frustration is Adler's designation for the personal feelings of suffering, sorrow and sin. It is "though a painful instrument...yet a necessary instrument of spiritual development."[39] None of us will escape frustration, for none of us can avoid becoming victims of "incompatibilities." Husband and wife will sometimes grow apart. Children and parents will differ. Master and apprentice will come to a parting of the ways. Given these and like experiences, frustration can lead to anger, to surrender, to separation, to dismissal. But it can also be an ethical experience and so a goad to reconstruction. "The doctrine which I am teaching seems to me to apply preeminently in the case of suffering...Suffering is a passive state; the cure of suffering is action."[40]

In fact, without awareness of the uses of frustration, it becomes all the more painful because all the more pointless. Adler's view of marriage illustrates his position,

> To the argument of those who hold that married people often do not find in each other invitations to enter into a more spiritual union...I answer that if we are not satisfied with one another as we are we have the power of remaking one another....[S]uccess in marriage depends upon...[seeing] the latent, the unapparent good in the other and [building] it up...and [calling] forth the golden possibilities that are hidden in every truly human soul....[41]

In his practice as an Ethical Culture Leader, therefore, Adler would not perform a wedding ceremony for any divorced man or woman. From his point of view, divorce is a confession of ethical passivity, and recognizing it is to enter into an unethical conspiracy. The failure to build up the unapparent good in the other is a victory of value over worth, a denial of the potency of self and other and so even a form of sacrilege.

No doubt, Adler's rigidity and absolutism are in part an expression of his culture and his time. By contrast, he is no less concerned but surely not as inflexible when it comes to institutions like the schools and experiments in social reform. With his notion of failure, he makes clear that he appreciates the gap between empirical and ideal. Error is likely, and not all error can be corrected. But marriage is different. On Adler's behalf, it can be argued that just as child and parent can never really sever their relationship, so husband and wife cannot either. The accident of the blood tie should not overshadow the moral connection, nor should biology be supreme over spirit.

"Bereavement" is another moment of frustration. Death, even when it is understood as "right farewell" and accepted as such, is nevertheless a moment of frustration for the dying who know they will lose the ability to pursue the ideal. This becomes all the more evident when death is surprising, unexpected and in a sense an intrusion. Adler's typical illustrations are the death of a young wife in the first year of marriage and the death of a child. But death is frustrating no matter when it occurs because it delivers the message that nothing really can any longer be done to continue the task of the ideal. Adler adds that it also communicates "the finitude of the human race itself." Death is thus a reminder that the species itself will vanish before the ideal is realized.

Adler, however, does not settle for retreat into sadness. For those who go on living, there is still moral possibility. Bereavement can be a time for strengthening life's relationships. Death, in other words, teaches both the living and the dying, and when they learn its lessons they have found a pathway toward consolation. In fact, Adler insists that contemplating the inevitable death of the human race makes the effort to perfect all present relationships all the more urgent. In a sense he is saying that even the species can be in a position of "right abdication." Immortality, then, is not an actual persistence of being, an indefinite extension of self in time, but an ideal relational characteristic which the spiritual manifold gives to the present. As such, however, immortality is neither the promise of heaven nor the threat of hell. A moment of movement toward the ideal is a moment of eternity, and in that sense immortality is simultaneous with mortality lived a certain way.

Society, obviously, presents us with its frustrations too. The trap of specialism, for example, is felt as such by the spiritualizing human being. The reformer learns of the ineffectiveness of his or her best efforts. But Adler is making a more subtle point than "try harder." He is, instead, asking the reformer to grasp the moral point of reform. When this is understood, then the present deserves its respect too and cannot be sacrificed for some future unconditioned and imagined good.[42] Given our limits as finite beings, the future, after all, need not necessarily be an improvement over the present. Adler, in other words, challenges the idle dream of utopia, a challenge he makes clear in an autobiographical comment.

> At this period (before 1890)...a species of millenialism for a time vitiated my thinking....I dallied with Utopias and flattered my imagination with the vision of something like a state of ultimate earthly felicity...the delusion did not last long....[43]

Reform, moreover, is too often contented with the appearance of change brought about by the anxiety of coming to grips with externalities. Certainly Adler understands the practical importance of social action and compromise and surely demonstrates these in his own institutional efforts. But Adler is no stoic, and he counsels against merely accepting the unchangeable. For him, the important things about us are in fact changeable. The self and its relationships are in our power. The reformer misses the point because he or she is compulsively attentive to the world out there. But reform is ultimately the changing of self, a matter of biography.

Reform, in turn, also leads to the third shadow, sin. Adler defines it as the consciousness of an evil act and its connections. For him, sin is a fact of moral psychology, and it is because of this location in the developing self that frustration arises. The evil act is a matter of moral judgment in the world of practices and certainly is not to be ignored. A sense of sin, however, is a characteristic of the ethicizing self. As a Roman Catholic critic of Adler remarks,

> Sin is to be carefully distinguished from evil but the distinction is almost the reverse of the ordinary one. Sin is opposed to what is intrinsically right, but the knowledge that the harmful deed is sinful comes to the sinner after the act....[As Adler writes,] "A man *can* knowingly commit evil but cannot with full consciousness commit sin...."[44]

The distinction reflects Adler's description of the development of the soul and his awareness of the pervasiveness of moral failure. Acts of violation are inevitable not just because there are villains out there but because the world is filled with conflicting obligations. But the rational being cannot knowingly choose to sin; that would be irrational. Yet conflicts do occur, and evil acts do occur. The consciousness of sin is therefore unavoidably painful. It follows then that sin is a feature of spiritual development and has two components, the act as such and the consciousness of its implications for the self. The latter, however, does not become clear, is not realized, until the act unfolds and is judged amidst its connections.

Adler, of course, is wrestling with the problem of the moral evil that good people do. Among the difficulties is the fact that self-knowledge is always imperfect, and so the awareness of the evil act as evil must come after the deed. Thus it is that with some exceptions the admission of an evil act is accompanied by a denial that in the instance it is evil and by a moral justification which, as uttered, is not merely rationalization. Evil may be admitted but not felt. Thus even moral judgment may be mechanistic and impersonal. Or the evil act may be excused by helplessness. Nearly everyone, in other words, claims the "good will." The moral import of an evil act, then, is not found in its status or in its external consequences but in its effects on the person and in its meaning for his or her future.

The past cannot be changed. So Adler's view of sin reflects his interest in a pedagogy of the soul. We may learn from what we have done in order to change what we yet will do. But, more significantly, as we learn we are changed not only in action but in moral development. And frustration arises precisely because, no matter how well we learn from ethical experience, the world is not ideal. Our moral education, therefore is always inadequate. Experience is a stubborn thing. Sin, therefore, is persistent. In his own way, Adler is reconstructing the notion of original sin. It is neither a fixed characteristic of human nature nor is it a punishment for defying God. Rather, it is another sign of ethical experience.

Adler is concerned not just with the admission of guilt but with the acceptance of responsibility. Confession does not succeed because it is a passive and even an egoistic response to the sense of sin. Remedial action, then, must make up for the evil act. But that action can only make moral sense if it finds a place in the emerging identity of the self. Otherwise acts of atonement, redress and reform remain superficial, and evil acts are reduced to violations of a rule or a code. Paradoxically, "sinning" is a sign of the way toward self awareness as a being to whom worth can be attributed.

Sin is a feature of personal experience. Adler thus rejects the crucified Christ as he does the notion of martyrdom and sacrifice because it is not really possible for anyone to live or die for another's sins. As Robert Guttchen remarks,

> An obligation which is indefeasible is such that one cannot be relieved of it by another....The locus of obligation in such matters lies wholly within the individual....And since an obligation of a person who has worth is also inalienable, it is neither possible for that person to turn over the obligation to someone else nor would it be proper for anyone to seek to take over someone else's responsibilities...no one can ethically live someone else's life and no one should try....[45]

Adler's distinction between sin and evil has its source and its justification in ethical experience. So, for example, it is possible for someone else to provide remedies for my evil act, as in paying my fine, substituting himself or herself for me in order take my punishment, etc. But it is not possible for me to transfer my sense of sin to another, although I may succeed in suppressing it. Sin is unique to each individual. Spiritual democracy, in other words, has its price. In particular, it does not legitimize the transfer of moral obligation. Indeed, to do so is to de-personalize obligation and so to invite authority to replace personality. As it were, although the child is in a state of "rightful subjection," the democratic citizen cannot be in that state and remain a citizen.

Once again, the personal and the social are entwined. Adler moves between them as different perspectives on a single reality. For example, in a comment on his vocation he says,

> The person qualified to be a religious leader is one who has ceased to make scapegoats of the worst offenders that merely exemplify on a larger scale the spirit dormant or active in all....He is impressed with the racial quality in moral evil...and it is at this point that he would apply to himself and others jointly the remedy....[46]

Consciousness of evil, like bereavement and failure, is an instrument for increasing and intensifying our relationships. Thus, the three shadows are essential to the soul's achievement.

Toward Self Consciousness

Character, as we have seen, is a restatement in biographical form of Adler's ideas of worth and membership in the spiritual manifold. It finds its fullest expression in Adler's thinking about schooling. Brought up in the Germanic tradition of *bildung*, the idea of character formation is quite natural to his educational thinking. At the same time, he is a progressive and so must marry a traditional and a radical idea. As John Dewey put the same point, "We cannot overlook the factors of discipline and characterbuilding...training in habits of order...and in the idea of industry....[47] Like Dewey, Adler reconstructs character formation in the light of new knowledge about child development and new attitudes toward schooling. The task is "...building up...the profoundly difficult task of supplying a working philosophy of life without traveling into the field of metaphysics...."[48]

Reconstruction, therefore, includes destruction. Again, Adler's educational thought provides the example.

> [T]here is one duty which we owe to our children, to tell them the truth....No matter how comforting a lie may be you have no business to tell it to your child....Every child has a right to profit by the experience of the past....You say, "It will not hurt the child. It will outgrow these beliefs just as I have outgrown them." Why should you put your child in the position of outgrowing anything? Why not let its development be normal and sane from the start?[49]

Adler needs to free education from moralism and mythology. Thus, honesty about what we know and do not know, about our departures from as well as our reverence toward traditions. Of course, there must be a "certain tenderness" toward the young. But it is not exhibited by comforting lies. It is self evident, Adler would say, that character formation demands truth-telling. A notion of "two truths," even when reduced to a strategy of development, is inconsistent with organicism.

Adler is also responding to modernist and liberal religious attempts to reconcile Genesis and Darwin, Scripture and science. In setting up a wall between them as a method of reconciliation, truth is finally lost. The consequence is that religion founders on metaphysics and secularity founders on superficiality. Character formation is thus a way of avoiding the mistake of the progressives by recognizing the truth of the soul. And it is a way of avoiding the mistake of tradition by recognizing the truth of the soul's development as an ethical personality. For truth, the heart of the matter is a direct encounter with the world as it is and with people as they are. But to be is also to become. What I am and what the world is includes their potentiality. So, Adler remarks,

> a religious society has no choice but to be an educational institution....The word education suggests a school house, class rooms, text books, laboratories...Why should such things arouse enthusiasm...dedication, sacrifice?...[Go] far down to something that is latent in the depths of human nature...what I have called...the Sublime, the capacity for the infinite....And this it is really the purpose of a genuine education...to draw out....[50]

The need, therefore, is for a reconstructed education. For Adler, the idealist as progressive, the child is an independent being and not just a proto-being in preparation. He or she has the capacities appropriate to where he or she is along life's way, "an idea brought into focus," says Adler, "in Rousseau's *Emile*." The integrity of childhood is, of course, the point of progressivism in all its forms. The kindergarten, the child-centered curriculum, teacher training and developmental psychology are its keynotes. But for Adler, classicism and tradition cannot be simply displaced. Instead, classicism must be progressive too. Adler thus mediates between the traditional and the modern. To become a partisan of one or the other, as so many of his contemporaries were doing, is to truncate education.

Inherited classicism contents itself with out-dated models falsely understood as eternal. Modernism makes method an end in itself and reduces philosophy to psychology. "The question for us today to whom education has become a religion is, can we accept not only the methods...but...the ideal....Now the broad and generous culture which enables a man to appreciate the best that is produced in all the arts and sciences...that is harmonious development....[51] Skill demands the complement of appreciation.

Reconstruction as metaphor and method stands Adler in good stead as he addresses the school as a project. Just adding on this or that subject to make a new education will not do the trick. Nor can the industrial problem be solved by mere modernism, by replacing education with training. Adler, in effect, is integrating ethical and industrial requirements. The outcome is to be the personality that is realizing itself by its competence in the marketplace.

To be sure, Adler assumes the possibility of a harmonious social universe where the emerging ethical personalities and the developing industrial skills can be coherently joined. These may, however, turn out to be in conflict. Industrialism may indeed demand the continuing evolution of mechanism and specialism for its survival. And the personality may need a kind of expressivism and individuality that cannot meet industrial needs. But, this is going to be evident, if at all, only in a future where the ideal has been tried out as *telos*. Adler's sense of the disarray of industrial culture warrants the risk. At the same time, his realism and pragmatism are its counterpoint. In practice, in other words, he was far less given to *a priori* solutions and much more likely to be experimental and tentative.

Adler comes close to expressing his pragmatism explicitly when he comments, typically, "we have got to get hold. We are born into a certain civilization. We want to get hold of it and understand it and add to it."[52] Like other progressives, then, he understands the limits of the idea when taken as an abstraction, as theory, particularly in the volatile atmosphere of the school and among the young.

"Getting hold" means keeping current with the empirical discoveries of the sciences. For example, Adler writes,

Perhaps the most signal advance in education...has been due to the discovery that the mind is tenanted from the outset. People used to treat the mind of the child as if it were an empty house into which knowledge could enter...[but] even the brain of the baby ...is already tenanted and all knowledge that wants to enter must...present a proper letter of introduction...knowledge must behave like a gentleman....[N]o two human minds are alike....[T]he moment it becomes evident that [the system] does not fit the living child...let your system go every time....[53]

To "let the system go" of course is the mark of experimentalism. At the same time, it is a criticism of classicism.

Unfortunately, the "new" education as Adler calls the progressive movement, has its own error. Its recognition of individuality and the uniqueness of persons has deteriorated into a disconnected individualism. Thus, it is corrupted by a loss of continuity, a loss of traditional values like loyalty and community. But the individual is still social and historical. The progressive curriculum is also tempted to lose the integrity of the subject matter. Its concern with student motivation and psychological development deteriorates into sensationalism. And the progressive's commitment to psychological readiness can lead to superficiality and to a neglect of thoroughness and discipline. Classicism, then is a necessary corrective.

Adler's synthesis of progressive and classic ideas is focused on the talent which is both a vocational and an educational idea. This shows up clearly when we examine his picture of what the school must become.

> [W]e must have a new kind of school...it is to be a grand experimental laboratory for testing every child that enters it, for discovering what its special talent may be.. .The teacher is told that...he must take account of the individual capacity of each pupil. But this kind of individualization still presupposes a general scheme into which the minds of all the pupils must be fitted....[I]ndividualization...should follow the nature of the pupil and not do violence to it in any way....[54]

The progressive's attention to "individual needs" makes sense to Adler only as it is corrected by the ideal. Like the other sciences, psychology can only take us so far.

Adler softens the image of the laboratory which runs into the danger of treating student and teacher as experimental objects. Thus, the religious idea is its correlative. The school is also a place in which to live. "The school should be to the pupil not an intellectual drill ground but a second home..." This image of the school as home is subtly different from Dewey's notion of the school as community. No doubt, it partly reflects Adler's Hebraism. In Judaism, the place for education is called, *bet,* and the same word is used for the location of family and of worship. Together with *bildung* and inquiry, the home plays a strategic role in Adler's reconstruction. As a home, the school brings to mind personal relationships.

Moral education which should begin in the earliest years brings "life axioms" to consciousness. The teacher, like the parent and religious leader, is however a moral personality in progress too. Vocationally, that personality shapes and is shaped by the relationship to the emerging personality of the student. It is not enough to teach only the group, the class, only the maxims and subjects. Ultimately the method is the masterapprenticeship relationship from which performance in class and with colleagues evolves. The moral educator, indeed all educators, cannot forget his or her own development. So, he or she "should take an interest in at least some one youth younger than himself who for lack of opportunity is not receiving the right education...should treat him as if he were a brother...."[55] And, returning to this theme year later he adds, "The right educator does certainly love his pupils. Does he ever look into the glass to catch their images as they are like to be in the future?"[56]

Finally, Adler's views on so called extracurricular activity emphasize the vocation of the teacher and the lifeencompassing image of the home. A mere collection of subject matters will not do with sports, hobbies and arts put to one side as secondary options after the important work of schooling is done. In fact, there is really nothing extracurricular at all if the school is to serve the moral ideal. If character is the end, then education is inclusive of experience and ideal as well.

Notes

[1] Adler was surely aware of Kant's discussion of the goal of education. The concern with character was its central theme.

> Our ultimate aim is the formation of character. Character consists in the firm purpose to accomplish something and then, also, in the actual accomplishing of it....The character of the wicked man is evil; but then, in this case we do not call it "character" any longer but obstinacy....

Immanuel Kant, *On Education*, translated by Annette Churton, Ann Arbor, University of Michigan Press, 1960, pp. 98-99.

[2] John Dewey, *Intelligence in the Modern World*, edited by Joseph Ratner, New York, Random House, 1939, pp. 410-411.

[3] Adler, "Third Lecture," Plymouth, p. 5.

[4] Felix Adler, "The Spiritual Basis of Reconstruction, address, January 5, 1919, pp. 7-8.

[5] Ralph Waldo Emerson, "The American Scholar," *The Complete Writings of Ralph Waldo Emerson*, New York, William H. Wise, 1929, p. 25.

[6] For Adler's comments on his relationship to Emerson, see, *An Ethical Philosophy*, pp. 27-29.

[7] Karl Marx on "Alienation Under Capitalism," cited in *Man Alone*, edited by Eric and Mary Josephson, New York, Dell, 1962, p. 63.

[8] Adler, *An Ethical Philosophy*, pp. 69-70.

[9] Alfred North Whitehead, *The Aims of Education*, New York, Mentor Books, 1949, p. 26.

[10] George Herbert Mead, "The Social Self," *Selected Writings*, edited by Andrew J. Reck, New York, Library of Liberal Arts, 1964, pp. 142-143.

[11] William James, *The Varieties of Religious Experience*, New York, Mentor, 1958, pp. 292-293.

[12] *The New York Times*, April 26, 1933, interview at the time of Adler's death.

[13] Ruth Pilpel Brickner, a practicing psychiatrist. From an interview cited by Howard B. Radest in *Toward Common Ground*, New York, Ungar, 1969, p. 105. I would add that while Adler certainly knew of Freud's work, there is scarcely a mention of him in his notes and to my knowledge no direct reference to him at all in Adler's published work.

[14] Recent work in psychology, psychiatry and psychoanalysis in part corroborates Adler's suspicions. For example, Erich Fromm joins his Humanism and Marxism to psychoanalysis in *The Sane Society* (New York, Rinehart and Company, 1955), Erik Erikson works out the "ethical implications of psychoanalytic insight" in *Insight and Responsibility* (New York, W. W. Norton and Company, 1964), and Lawrence Kohlberg integrates John Rawls "theory of justice" with cognitive psychology in *Essays in Moral Development*, Vol. 1, *The Philosophy of Moral Development* (San Francisco, Harper and Row, 1981).

[15] Phillip Rieff, *The Triumph of the Therapeutic*, New York, Harper and Row, 1966, p. 149.

[16] For example, see Thomas Kuhn's classic study, *The Structure of Scientific Revolutions*, Chicago, University of Chicago Press, 1970.

[17] Felix Adler, "The Problem of Teleology," *International Journal of Ethics*, XIV, 1904, pp. 278-279.

[18] Mead, *Selected Writings*, p. 145.

[19] Adler develops this theme carefully in "Goethe's Social Ideal," address, December 3, 1905.

[20] Adler, *Religion of Duty*, pp. 122-124.

[21] Adler, "Goethe's Social Ideal," p. 4. It is interesting to re-read this address in the light of modern experience. In his discussion of *Wilhelm Meister*, Adler raises the question of the "role" as "pose" and points to the development of the role as an alienated behavior that is not recognized as alienating.

[22] Adler, "Goethe's Social Ideal," *passim*.

[23] Felix Adler, "Spiritual Self Education," address, December 16, 1923, pp. 12-13.

[24] William James, *The Principles of Psychology*, New York, Henry Holt, 1890, Volume I, pp. 237-238.

[25] Felix Adler, "Oxford Lecture on Education," Philosophy Club Notes, 1923, pp. 13-14.

[26] Adler, *An Ethical Philosophy*, pp. 52-53.

[27] Felix Adler, "The Relation of the Moral Ideal to Reality," *International Journal of Ethics*, Vol. XXI, 1911, pp. 7-8.

[28] Adler, "The Relation of the Moral Ideal to Reality," p. 8.

[29] Edmond Cahn, *The Moral Decision*, Bloomington, Indiana University Press, 1955.

[30] In a conversation that I had with Horace Friess on the subject, he said that Adler used this term to challenge much of traditional mysticism while accepting the designation, "mystic" for himself.

[31] Adler, *Reconstruction*, pp. 194-195.

[32] Felix Adler, "Ethical Development Extending Through Life," address, Second International Congress on Moral Education, The Hague, 1912.

[33] Adler, "Eighth Lecture," Plymouth, p. 3.

[34] Adler, "Eighth Lecture," Plymouth, pp. 11-12.

[35] Adler, "Eleventh Lecture," Plymouth, p. 8.

[36] The theme of life's "ethical" stages is developed in Adler's lecture at the Second International Congress on Moral Education, "Ethical Development Extending Through Life." My comments refer to that document.

[37] Adler, *An Ethical Philosophy*, p. 304n.

[38] Adler, "Ethical Development Extending Through Life," pp. 18-19.

[39] Adler, *An Ethical Philosophy*, p. 153.

[40] Adler, *The Religion of Duty*, pp. 165-166.

[41] Adler, "Fifth Lecture," Plymouth, p. 18.

[42] For a discussion of this theme, see *An Ethical Philosophy*, Chapter V, "Social Reform, pp. 43-57.

[43] Adler, *An Ethical Philosophy*, p. 42.

[44] Samuel Frederick Bacon, *An Evaluation of the Philosophy and Pedagogy of Ethical Culture*, Washington, D.C., Catholic University, 1933, p. 19n. Citation is from *An Ethical Philosophy*, p. 172.

[45] Robert S. Guttchen, *An Identification, Analysis and Evaluation of Felix Adler's Ethics and Philosophy of Education*, dissertation, New York University, 1962, p. 35. Later, after Guttchen's accidental death, a revision of the dissertation was published as *Felix Adler*, New York Twayne Publishers, 1974.

[46] Felix Adler, "A New Type of Religious Leader," *Ethical Addresses* XVII, 1912, p. 218.

[47] Dewey, *Dewey on Education*, pp. 36-37.

[48] Adler, *An Ethical Philosophy*, pp. 58-59.

[49] Felix Adler, "The Religious Education of Children," undated address but probably given prior to 1895, p. 5.

[50] Felix Adler, "The Ethical Ideal of Education," address, November 15, 1926, pp. 1-2.

[51] Felix Adler, "The New Education, Its Triumphs and Defects," address, April 29, 1900, pp. 9-10.

[52] Adler, "The New Education," p. 11.

[53] Adler, "The New Education," pp. 7-8.

[54] Adler, "The New View of Childhood," pp. 12-13.

[55] Adler, "Twelfth Lecture," Plymouth, p. 13.

[56] Adler, "First Lecture on Culture," p. 1.

V

CULTURE AND POLITICS

Power

> ...a flower grows; it is a living thing; and all its parts are alive. So is society a living thing.[1]

Adler's mysticism leads him to the emerging and self conscious self and from it to society. His prophetic temperament turns him toward society and from it to the self. For both mystic and prophet, the common enemy is mechanistic behavior, e. g., the de-personalized priest acting the role in someone else's drama of salvation; the bureaucrat functioning to industrial specifications. The mystic condemns the crippling of personality by externality. The prophet defies a society that destroys the human relation. In Adler, these voices have in common a passion for the ideal and a sense of the fruitfulness of ethical experience as the bridge between both inspirations.

Adler's idealism, as we have seen, takes hold of the self through the process of an ethical education, an education guided toward a society of ends by the idea of worth. An ethically educated man or woman reaches toward his or her identity but never quite makes it. He or she helps to shape the souls of others who in turn reach back to help in shaping him or her. It is out of Adler's mysticism, indeed a socialized mysticism, that an education, properly called religious, is developed. The prophet in him adds that education is also political education. Religion and politics are two ways of seeing the same ethical being. The former attends to an end *per se*, the latter to a society of ends. At the same time, religion and politics are themselves forms of culture and have an educational mission. The ethical ideal is learned in the relationships of soul with soul and in the acts of person with person

Adler's vision, therefore, is both unitary and bi-focal. Character and society are not inevitably at war with each other. I am not, as Reinhold Niehbuhr put it, condemned to live as a "moral man in an immoral society." Indeed, where self and society are at war, ethical experience delivers the message of a failing character in a failing society. The undeveloped self and the unethical society are implications of each other. The task then is again reconstruction, now a reconstruction of education as a politics.

Surely the state of society as it is...throws no light upon the question of
society as it ought to be...I say that a school which has merely supplied
the pupil with the ability to get the means of living leaves him quite
uninstructed...because we cannot truly live without a commanding
purpose in life...to create a new society and ourselves as members of it.
Ever and ever anew...to re-create society and to re-create ourselves as
members of it.[2]

Adler, always the philosopher in the marketplace, is not only
responding to political corruption but to the faddism of the "new"
education as it makes it way from originators like Dewey and Mead
into popular and professional discourse.   Slogans like "life
adjustment" and pseudo-scientific language like "socialization" also
seem to address the political question, the social question, *i. e.,* seem to
see education as politics.   But they turn progressivism away from the
ethical ideal and toward the prudential.   Such language betrays the
sentimentality and even the ultimate and unwitting conservatism of the
progressive.   As against it, "Nobility and not happiness is the
evolutionary end...a society in which personalities shall have become
transformed."[3]

Of course, politics is, in Adler's sense, not the give and take of
the clubhouse nor the maneuvers for the partisan advantage of the
party.   Adler is, if you will, working with an Aristotelian notion, a
classical notion.   Reflecting on Greece and Rome, politics is an
architectonic discipline giving shape and purpose to the human being
as sociable being.   Its arena and end is the *res publica,* the public
good.   But ethically understood, the public good necessarily entails
the personal and private good as well.   In discussing it, Adler
addresses himself specifically to the one actual society which evokes
his personal loyalty.   His political question, then, is how can America
be reconstructed to achieve the public good, how can it recapture the
genius of its origins in the midst of industrial transition?   Neither the
American imperium nor the "American Century" is the American
dream.   Founded as a new nation in the new world, America is the
present occasion of the ethical future of human society itself.   Much is
at stake in the reconstruction.   The Abraham Lincoln influence of
Adler's childhood persists.

In order to develop a context for his reconstruction of the
American mission, Adler applies the metaphor of vocation to the
national and international scene.   So, each nation has its vocation, its
talent, and thus its contribution to make to the development of the
human race.   Taken in concert, all nations, ethically conceived, join in

a "functional internationalism," much as the reconstruction of religion, work and school lead to similarly patterned functionalities. Organism remains Adler's heuristic model. Of course, in the never to be completed struggle between worth and value, each nation must fall short of its vocation, and this is not only its domestic but its global failure. In so far as any nation is worthy of loyalty, however, it is because of its indispensable participation in the orchestration of humankind as social being. Reconstruction, then, is the patriot's obligation. So Adler, nurtured on the Americanism of Emerson, Lincoln and Jefferson sees the political question for the American as a question of its normative ideal, its talent for democracy.

A nation, like a person, has its genius. Thus, the normative ideals of the German, the English, the Japanese are necessarily different from the American. But unlike most other nations whose genius has a less universal intention in the modern world, the special mission of the American in this orchestration is to bring to global realization the notion of spiritual democracy. It is not mere coincidence that puts America on the scene as industrial society is emerging. Just as industrialism changes the nature of boundaries, so America has its boundlessness too. With examples in mind like the civilizing influences of classical Greece and Rome, of the England of the seventeenth century, of the France of the eighteenth century or of the Germany of the nineteenth century, America's claim to loyalty is global, and its object is larger than the nation alone.

Only for the American nation in an industrial society is the globe itself encompassed. Because of this, loyalty is an ethical claim. The development of democracy everywhere, the American mission, is a necessary condition for personal development too. American exceptionalism thus takes an ethical turn for Adler, the urgency of its reconstruction in a global industrial setting of the legal and political universalism of the Declaration of Independence and the Bill of Rights. America's vocation is to set an example and so to exhibit the realistic possibility of the move toward the moral ideal. It serves as a standard and so offers a measure of each nation's achievements and failures, including the actual achievements and failures of the American Republic itself. Adler, then, is not defending America for its own sake, nor is he calling for it to lead a crusade. Imitation for nations as for individuals is the enemy of the talent. Adler is a radical pluralist in his patriotism too.

Reconstruction requires vision, agency and power. For Adler, taking a leaf from the realist's book, politics is the organization and use of power. But, power is ideally conceived as the capacity to effect moral change. In that sense, high office and great wealth do not necessarily assure power at all. They may even be signs of delusion, even of powerlessness.

> We must plead against the present system not in the interest of the under-
> dog alone but in the interest also of those who seem to be victors in the
> struggle.[4]

The question of power is not simply one of control, of "vested" interests or of getting what one wants. The end to be achieved is an ethical end. The ethical quality of the means to that end cannot be ignored either. Of course, persons in power argue that they are by no means powerless. That is the error and perhaps even the sour grapes, they might say, of the theorist and the reformer. More cynically, they might also add that it is the position of an outsider, of someone who does not know the pleasures of authority and status. Adler, of course, would agree that even the "illusions of power" have their rewards. Value, after all, is not without its pleasures. But he might also point out that power so conceived is always insecure, even paranoid. There is no moment of satisfaction and no resting place. The possessor of this illusory power is always looking over his or her shoulder.

The political realist in Adler might well note that in an interdependent society, an industrial society, everyone is powerless and powerful to the same or nearly the same degree. Few if any can achieve their ends, can make a difference. Opposition, the social veto, is becoming more widely available than every before. As we know and as Adler could only guess, small groups, even lone individuals, can sabotage social institutions. Stopping traffic or occupying a building or blowing up an airplane are strategies of paralysis. In Adler's time, the industrial strike or the act of violence prevents positive achievement. His references include events like the Pullman strike and the Haymarket riots. Ironically, in an industrial society, power increases but is nameless and negative. So under the rule of value, powerlessness increases at the same time.

Adler, of course, is not surprised that an organism needs the cooperative participation of all its members. Indeed, that is the point of an ethical criticism of industrial politics. It is not simply corrupt but ineffective and likely to become more so. Therefore, it is on the grounds of both idealism and practice that compromise turns out to be ethical. Thus, even compromise has its reconstruction. Its moral terms are reciprocal adjustment, mutuality and cooperation. Give and take have different faces when seen with the opposing perspectives of value and worth. Failure, falling short of the ideal, is common to all human beings and to all societies. And success is common too. This partiality of achievement and failure is a recognition of the social need, the moral need, of human beings for each other. So the notion of the talent, of the indispensable contribution of each to all, is the source of an ethical theory of compromise. In that way, the ideal provides a standard for distinguishing between compromise and opportunism. A nuanced judgment in the world is, of course, always necessary. Principle, as in legalism and rationalism, can be become mechanistic too.

Power relies on competence and nowhere more obviously than in industrial society. Thus, the connection between specialty, vocation, and power. The Baconian motto, "knowledge is power," becomes the essence of power in an industrial society. To be sure, the societies of the Christian middle ages enjoyed their own connection between knowledge and power. Thus the Church claimed the pathway to salvation and so justified its political potency. The knowledges of trade and military skill surely had no small effect on the powers of Athens and Rome. But in an industrial society knowledge is more comprehensive and, in a secular world, more visible and effective. That is the intention of science and technology and is well illustrated by the developing role of the technical expert and the professional.

Under the rule of value, however, the specialist is trapped in specialism and so knowledges are subverted by disconnection from each other and by disconnection from the ideal. Thus, what could be powerful in the interests of democracy becomes instead another adjunct to political habits and institutions, to the merely present. The expert becomes another hired hand, an adjunct to inherited status or to acquired wealth. Consequently, political expectations are frustrated. On the one hand, there is the manifest availability of knowing how to do more and more about more and more. On the other hand, there is the increase of misdirected achievement and mal-distributed goods. The citizen cries out, "do something." The official answers, if at all, "I'm trying." Institutions tend to become ungovernable, and power yields to ritualistic behavior, as in Fourth of July celebrations. Here and there, of course, persons in power enjoy its perquisites. But intentional social evolution surrenders to inertia. At the same time, the veto appears also as the repressive power of governments and other collective institutions. They can easily say "no," but are helpless to achieve. Nearly everyone confesses helplessness. The isolation of competence and ideal leads to disaster.

Too many of the reformers fail to grasp the organic, the ethical, import of the relationship of power and competence. Thus, rather than address the question of *telos*, they act under the illusion that successful effort here and there will eventually bring about the good society. Reform, in other words, is also caught in specialism. Technique, mere process without end, is substituted for knowledge. In a sense, this is to carry over into reform Adam Smith's "invisible hand." The specialist becomes the mere expert who is treated and who treats himself or herself as a vehicle for a skill that has, in effect, been de-personalized. Education itself reflects this phenomenon and becomes only utilitarian. Thus it fails to meet the moral requirements of power.

> ...[O]ur educational system, despite certain advantages, is pointless. I have traced over-specialization back to provisionalism...[however] we can advance educational theory and practice by setting the example of a teleological education system.[5]

To be sure, advances do happen. But progress in this or that is neither inevitable nor necessarily coherent. Indeed, one advance can easily cancel out another.

Adler, as we know, is a political activist and a successful political reformer.[6] He is surely in touch with the politics and the politicians of his day. He sees the evolution of the political machine. As a young man, he is witness to the corruptions of Tammany locally and of the Grant administration nationally. But he also knows that while "power may tend to corrupt," powerlessness is just as corrupting. Thus, Adler's analysis is three-fold. The illusion of power, its appearance as status and possessions, may be enjoyable but is ultimately an admission that its possessor is in the power of someone or something else. The opportunism of power is essentially negative as more and more people realize the availability of the veto. And the power of knowledge informed by *telos*, which is the power of the cultured human being in a cultured society, awaits reconstruction. Culture is a process of social energy and social effectiveness. It appears when organic images replace mechanical ones, when, for example, expertise is corrected by awareness of the reciprocal radiation between any one specialty and all other specialties.

> The moral ideal is a social ideal....It is the ideal of a spiritual whole, each member of which expresses uniquely some aspect of the life of the whole, is sustained by the whole and sustains it and is indispensable to it. The moral ideal is that of a multiple god, a commonwealth of spirits, not of one spirit who, as sovereign, stands apart and aloof and to whom the rest are subject....The theistic conception is monarchical, the conception here indicated is democratic.[7]

Character formation comes to wear a political costume. The emerging personality, interacting with other personalities, is the agent of ethical change and is, in turn, changed. The purpose of power, then, is the creation of conditions under which personalities can emerge. Social reform thus has a spiritual mission,

> ...[T]he task of what is often loosely called "social reform" (is) to create the ethical series...the family, the school, the state, the international society...."[S]ocial reform" is strictly correct only when used comprehensively in this way. To confine its usage to the more equitable repatriation of wealth or to changes in economic conditions is unwarrantably too narrow....Social reform is *the reformation of all the social institutions in such a way that they may become successive phases through which the individual shall advance toward the acquisition of an ethical personality.*[8]

Politics, then, is to deal with subjects and not with objects, and the citizen is the end *per se* in the political arena. To make this happen, religion has its obligation too and is not simply to be dismissed. It retains its ancient form. It stands for transcendent purpose even in the modern world. But, it must now take on an industrial and democratic content. Thus Adler writes, "The great task of the Church today is to develop and proclaim a new social ideal...to interpret the conception of *Civitas Dei* in such a way as to express the aspirations of our age...."[9] Religion needs its own reconstruction, and this, in its way, is the motive for Adler's Ethical Culture Societies. Like education, religion finds its way into the marketplace.

Jefferson Re-visited

It is difficult for us to appreciate the idealism which once seemed so natural to America and the American. For us, all too often, class interest hides behind democratic rhetoric, and self-serving nationalism is cloaked by democratic crusade. But Adler finds idealism less difficult than we do, and not just because he lives before a time of mass media, political manipulation, urban decay and a growing underclass. Of course, he is not blind to the betrayal of the American dream by "manifest destiny" and "dollar diplomacy." Indeed, he is among the first and most active critics of our imperialism in the Philippines and Latin America.[10] Adler is to be counted, too, among those who very early condemned racism as a global and national disgrace. Among others, W. E. B. DuBois and Booker T. Washington were speakers on the Ethical Society's Sunday Platform, and Adler's colleagues, John Elliot, William Salter, Anna Garlan Spencer and Henry Moskowitz signed the call for forming the National Association of Colored People. Thus too, Adler's leadership of the International Races Congress. Yet, ever the realist, he does not surrender the ideal,

> ...[I]n this rough democracy of ours, there is after all one...fundamental ethical principle enshrined....[E]very human being is to count, the worth of the common man...(is thus) to evolve...the spiritual democracy [emerging] out of the rough democracy...to prepare [him or her] to take ...part in the task of changing the democracy of today, the poor pitiful thing it is, into the nobler thing which it may be.[11]

Adler's hopefulness is not the Enlightenment belief in the inevitability of progress. Good things are not just going to happen simply as a consequence of the universalism of science and rationality. The American must help progress happen. America is built on the ideal, the development of free persons and the non-assignable responsibility of the person for himself or herself and to others. Thus, "The American ideal is that of the uncommon quality latent in the common man. [I]t is an ethical...a spiritual ideal; otherwise it would be nonsense. For taking men as they are...the common man is uncommonly common...."[12] Precisely because this is so, Adler's criticism of America is even more radical and harsh. Our inadequacy is a moral failure and a global failure, and not narrowly an institutional or epistemological failure.

The American dream is a social ideal. For all the talk of individualism, the American has confidence in the moral power of communities. The town meeting and the voluntary association, the idea of neighborhood itself, are testimony to that confidence. No doubt, Adler reflects too the immigrant's image of America as the "golden land." Thus, in a revealing comment, he remarks,

> It is because of this subconscious ethical motive that there is this generous air of expectation in America, that we are always wondering what will happen next or who will happen next....For America differs from all other nations in that it derives its inspiration from the future....[13]

The strategic importance of education is all the more evident in this America of failure and potentiality. The "basic" skills, reading, writing and arithmetic, are no doubt important. But more important is the release of the talent, the nurture of each person's latency. For

Adler, American democracy is in itself an educational experience for all its members. Consequently, the democratic statesman or stateswoman must be an educator. Again, the classic influence is clear enough. Adler has in mind the Platonic "philosopher king" now reconstructed as the philosopher citizen. No doubt, too, he is reflecting on Thucydides' description of Pericles and on Rome's Cicero and Cincinnatus. Like the founders of the Republic, Adler has no difficulty in connecting the mission of the newest of nations with the inspiration of Greece and Rome, just as when at Cornell he connected the Hebrew prophets with the Declaration of Independence.

To be sure, every state educates its citizens. It does so as a matter of continuity and survival. But the American Republic educates for potentiality, for the unknown future and not just the hallowed past. With the secular industrial state, however, government itself becomes a specialty. So, education is left to teachers, law to lawyers and government to officials. Specialism wears a political costume. A reference to the classic example is a reminder of organicism in politics, and of the distinction between education and training.

Beyond specialism, the American state in action does what it would not have its citizens do. It violates its own ideal when it allows the poor to be exploited, the Black to be lynched, the Native American to be dispossessed and peoples to be colonized. Of course, a modern day Macchiavelli would recognize such an America. He would applaud its success in giving the appearance of virtue by clothing these acts and failures in the language of the American dream. And Adler would reply, no doubt, that as the dream is emptied of content, it sooner or later ceases to warrant loyalty and so, even on the realist's grounds, becomes unworkable.

Adler is very much the Jeffersonian with his concern for human rights and with his sense of the strategic centrality of schooling in a democracy. But America is no longer an agricultural society. In such a society, the work itself was not only an economic necessity but an education in skill and community. As Jefferson put it in his *Notes On Virginia*, planting and harvesting are the natural instruction of the citizen. A minimal government was then a sufficient government. Now, with the coming of industrial society, the gap opens wide between home and work, between person and community and between individual and society. In this new environment the common sense of the American Republic is eroded. It is not so much that the American is anti-intellectual, as the Europeans have it, but that in America's early years, the citizen had his or her intelligence nurtured in the daily experience. Now that is no longer the case, and the fragmentation and objectification of persons by the division of labor become the norms of the industrial system.

The new experience calls for ideological reconstruction and not just for practical effort. For the American dream to survive, its ideas must regain a living content.

> In the Declaration of Independence, Jefferson...put forth the astonishing proposition that human equality is self evident...the opposite is self evident....Since Jefferson's day the faces have markedly changed. We have passed the agricultural stage and have entered the stage of industrial development....the facts to which the Declaration...appealed have altered....In the United States...Negro lynchings, the conditions in the sweated industries, and the widespread evil of child labor show us clearly enough how little the doctrine of the intrinsic worth of man has as yet become the property of even the most advanced nations....[14]

Adler's idea of a vocational reconstruction of the state is thus a revision of democratic ideology. It provides the new content appropriate for the transition from compulsive independence toward global interdependence. Washington's advice about "entangling alliances" and Monroe's "doctrine" do not meet the modern condition. America now has the duty of its "radiations" outward to the world. Since for Adler matters are always reciprocal, America's debt to the world also needs to become part of the American's consciousness. Education has its role to play here too. The American population is a "nation of immigrants," and this, as it were, is also a curriculum. "Thus, both the humanitarian ideal and the actual make-up of the people betray a cosmopolitan tendency...."[15] To learn from the industrial transition, to bring its ethical meaning to consciousness, is to make it an ethical experience in yet another way.

Industrializing American, in short, can no longer get away with "doing what comes naturally." A new era of intention and self-consciousness is needed. Once upon a time, the wedding of ideal and practice seemed to arise spontaneously in the coming together of rural communities and in the learnings of farm and field. Now, this wedding demands discipline and organization. Reconstruction, therefore, is not Jefferson's "revolution every twenty years." Indeed, industrial society could not survive revolution. Instead, the themes of the Declaration must be brought to new application under conditions of a mass society and the division of labor.

Education as a political act replaces revolution. This replacement follows from the interdependence of industrial society, which needs its continuities. In other words, revolution is inevitably a political, economic and social break with the past that industrialism cannot abide. Dislocation of the very apparatus of society itself would, in an impacted world, mean disaster. To justify revolution in a serious way, then, it would be necessary to show that industrialism itself ought to be destroyed. But for Adler, neither Luddite nor anarchist, the present is always an ethical experience and as such cannot be so naively dismissed. In other words, an industrial system calls for a new politics, an education as a politics.

The revolutionary, moreover, cannot avoid self-consciousness. In fact, revolution's claim is always a moral claim. So, he or she must be aware of the radiations of the revolutionary vocation itself. The idea of worth, then, can justify the overthrow of industrial society only in the limiting case, only *in extremis*.[16] In practice, particularly in a democratic and industrial society, revolution would seem to be rarely available as a justifiable option. It would be necessary for the revolutionary to argue for the beneficent effects of his or her action on those deposed and on those on the side lines. Nor can this be simply a claim about some future and unknown good. Moreover, the likelihood of violation has its reciprocal effect on the violator, the revolutionary. It is doubtful then, again except in the rarest of situations, that revolution is morally justifiable on Adler's grounds.

The reconstruction of education as a politics is therefore an urgent alternative, for reform is certainly necessary. Absent the effort and people will likely turn to their old self-destroying and now society-destroying habits. The issue of power, then, is not abstract, particularly as the American dream no longer matches reality. While freedom and equality remain as its ethical forms, a new historic occasion is in the making. To ethicize it, Adler turns to its richness as ethical experience. There, Adler's mysticism finds corroboration in a reconstructed American individualism as the social self. His prophetic temperament looks toward the American experience for institutional expression of the ethical ideal. To be sure, education is a characteristic form of politics in the Jeffersonian community. Now it becomes the moment for America's move into industrialism and onto a world stage.

The Reconstruction of Power

Universalism is an American tradition. Following the founders, the democratic revolution on this continent is for Adler, as it still is for many of us, is the forerunner of world reconstruction. Moving America from its rural past to its industrial future thus has global implication. At the same time, America's vision tempts an American imperialism. This takes shape not simply as a colonialism that does not confess what it is, but as the moral assumption that something is good just because the American says or does it. Spiritual imperialism, in other words, is also a result of the American dream. For Adler, the moralism of Wilson is but the most recent example of its appearance in the nation's *psyche*. As he puts it, "As President, it was his part to suggest something, not the ideal of the far future, but the next step that would lead in the ideal direction...." Instead, complains Adler, Wilson appeals to a "state of things that obtains nowhere."[17] Adler once again is at pains to exhibit his realism against "mere moralism." The relationship between what is and what ought to be cannot be severed. The ethical experience cannot be evaded.

In the "war to end wars," the danger of moralism is most clearly revealed. Ethics becomes abstract precisely when attention to the concrete is most necessary. Thus, Wilson's tenacious and even heroic fight for the League of Nations is, sadly, only formalism. The democratic talk of the "victors" covers their interest in reparations and territorial concessions. The "red scare" of the post-war period is not only a problem of civil liberty but a violation of persons. A moralistic rhetoric conceals, but surely does not serve, the moral ideal. In consequence, and most problematic of all, dishonesty is what the state educates its citizens sooner or later to expect. As it deals in moral lies, and as we catch on to what it is doing, the state loses its hold on us. Thus, an alleged realism does a disservice both to ethics and to practice. We become suspicious of all uses of power and all claims of virtue. We retire from the field.

For Adler, this is the deadly outcome of moralism. Because it teaches us that power is of necessity evil, it leaves power unreconstructed. To the contrary, as we have seen, for Adler power is implicit in the notion of worth itself. As Robert Guttchen remarks, "if a person had worth, he would be efficacious in his relations to other persons."[18] Adler's ethical imagery is characteristically filled with reference to effectiveness, change, control, direction and energy. Adler describes ethics as "actions and reactions" and "right energizing." He speaks of "organization as moralization." So his ethical idealism may be reformulated as a theory of power which in his ethical philosophy would stand in organic relationship to a theory of religion, a theory of education and a theory of work. As it were, these different attempts to reconstruct the present complete each other. Once again, an organic metaphor is at work.

The moral error is to treat power an end in itself, as disconnected from *telos*. But in fact power cannot be freely attached to any possible end. Means do shape our ends. To ignore this is the mistake of reading reality through the lens of value, of conceiving power mechanistically and after the image of interchangeable parts. Thus, we fall into the trap of isolating political, economic and moral power from each other. It is in that way that power corrupts. We are blinded to the moral fact that power too has its "radiations." When the mind is cleared of the mechanistic illusion, however, we realize that power can be ennobling and not simply manipulative, particularly when understood organically. No doubt, Adler has in mind the power that flows from the student who begins to realize his or her talent and so lives a new life through competence. He is recalling, too, the effects on the immigrant and slum dweller of economic and political accessibility. Above all, Adler is concerned to avoid the notion that evil is powerful and good inherently helpless. He rejects the sentimental notion that "the meek shall inherit the earth."

Like it or not, the soul lives in the marketplace. It cannot go untouched through the world. So the encounter with power is unavoidable. As with all ethical experience, the question is not whether to have it or not but what can be done with it. Power is never mere power. Failure to acknowledge this is to make the mistake of the religionist, the mistake of passivity. That is to play into the hands of those whose interests are served by keeping power and ideal apart, the opportunists, the self-seeking politicians and the "economic royalists." In isolating ethics and power, a false dualism between soul and world is perpetuated. Effectiveness is abdicated. Ethics becomes an empty exercise and religion a museum piece. Echoes of Adler's Temple sermon in 1873 and of his 1876 address are heard. Religion is to enter the market place, "deed" before "creed." Now for the mature Adler, however, the initiating moral criticism emerges as a philosophically developed idea.

Powerlessness inevitably produces a retreat from the ideal, a subversion of worth. The soul is made less and less capable of nurturing other souls. Hence, neither they nor it develop, and the talent remains only latent. Similarly, powerlessness takes shape as the disconnection between ethics and politics. Thus, the ethical choice is disarmed, unable to have its effects in the public arena. Historically, modernist ethics has indeed been resigned to abstraction and utopianism. A new Stoicism justifies all political acts, and ethics is reserved to a state of mind or state of soul. Utilitarianism lacks connection to ideal ends, and so converts ethics into prudence, in which case calculation replaces duty. And Kantianism divorces ethics and social history, leaving ethics without content and reducing it to an arid and lonely exercise of "pure practical reason."

Adler evokes the ethical imagination as the method of grasping moral power. Future experience is to validate present actions, although Adler's pragmatism is always referred to an ultimate end-in-view. Thus,

> The ethical rule applied to human relations is to treat chance relations as if they were necessary relations, to transform them into necessary relations; to treat a companion whom chance has associated with us as if he were indispensable to us in the attainment of the supreme end.[19]

The facts of the matter are important but not, as the realist would have it, an invitation to amorality. The ethical imagination does not float freely but is nourished by the contingent. Where we are born, what we inherit, what our community offers in the way of schooling and employment initiate personality. But these chance relations are to be worked on, to be re-worked, in the direction of distinctiveness of personality. As value is transformed in the direction of worth, other and unexpected relationships become available. Choices open up exhibiting previously inconceivable radiations and connections. In turn, these reflect back to open up yet new directions and choices for the personality. Freedom is, thus, the form of power, and freedom is made genuinely possible when the contingent is seized and converted. By contrast, those who are seen as in power remain victims of ambitions, of possessions, of compulsions. They are essentially unfree, essentially in the power of something other.

Adler also defends the ethical imagination against the supernatural. The fear of divine punishment and the hope of divine reward are, since Kant's "antinomies of pure practical reason," no longer available to the ethicist. In that sense, God is dead to Adler long before Nietzsche's aphorism becomes an existential argument for Protestant theology or post-modern atheism. Conscience remains, but it is rooted in the having of and learning from ethical experience. As Adler puts it,

> Sin remains whether you believe in a personal God or not, whether you believe you will be punished or rewarded in the hereafter or not...sin remains...as an injustice, as a wrong, as a transgression of an eternal law in things....It does not make any difference whether there is a God...I knew the thing was wrong and I did it....That is common sense, that is plain moral sense, that is the unsophisticated testimony of conscience.[20]

Adler, in developing a picture of the ethical imagination, is taking on both the traditionalist and the modernist. Against the former, he maintains that a wrong is a wrong not because God says so but because it violates the ideal. Hence, God is ethically redundant. Against the modernists like positivists and reductionists, Adler insists that wrongfulness has not lost its cognitive meaning. Ethics can still speak sensibly in its own name. Ethical experience, Adler notes, reveals the presence of moral categories in social relationships. The distinction between right and wrong is a precondition of law and of contract, as in truth telling and promise keeping. The relationships of husbands and wives, of employers and employees, of state and citizen, particularly when things go awry, depend on a shared sense of good and evil and particularly on a sense of fairness and its violation.

Mere conventionalism will not do. Conscience would then be only a name given to feelings about rules that may have functional utility but that could be changed by new conventions. Once convention is known as such, it is diminished by a sense of the arbitrary and loses its power. External force must be invoked and force always generates counter force. Hobbes, in other words, is back in the saddle. One way out, of course, is to hide the conventionality of convention, to develop a society which lives by generalizing the "royal lie." But apart from the riskiness of exposure, this approach puts untruth at the center of ethics, a paradoxical outcome that subverts the realist's claim to have an ethical philosophy or an adequate alternative to it.

A traffic-rule approach may work out well when nothing much is at risk, or when this or that way of behaving is indifferent to the outcome as long as it is commonly agreed to. But when ethics is taken seriously and when serious things are at stake, convention does not serve. The temptation to break the rule grows, and since the rule is external and merely conventional, it stirs little of a consciousness of sin and does not evoke moral shame. Ethics becomes quite literally powerless.

The reconstructionist in Adler, however, does not leave traditional approaches to simple rejection. After all, convention does build on the ethical notion of social agreement, and religion does point to the need for *sancta*. It is these, social agreement and inviolability, that are to be found in the center of an ethics of power. The appeal of power is to the achievement of ends, even attenuated ends like the enjoyments that flow from the illusions of power. But in an industrial society, repercussions are inevitable. No person is able to be powerful all alone, and no exercise of ordinary powers in politics and economics can long be hidden. Taking account of others in some way is a practical and a moral necessity. The real choice, then, is between the gamble that we can get away with overpowering or fooling the other and finding ways to coordinate with the other. Ultimately, on Adler's view, the harmonization of properly chosen ends is at least partially possible even in the world of value. A potential if not an actually coherent world order is presumed. Hence, the importance of converting "chance relations" into "necessary ones." The consciousness of connection is the hopeful sign that an ethics of power is invited by an industrial society.

Adler, of course, is not foolish enough to expect conflict simply to vanish. Thus, it too is to be reconstructed.

> So far from ruling out conflict, I regard conflict as a weapon of progress, an ethical weapon....Individuals and social classes too...learn to respect the rights which they find in practice they cannot traverse....But conflict is an ethical weapon only if it be wielded like the knife in the surgeon's hands....So should the battle of social reform be animated by concern not only for the oppressed but also for the oppressor...only that conflict which is waged...for the reasons of rescue of both the victim and the oppressor will attain its end.[21]

As it were, Adler proposes an ethical theory of confrontation. An ethics of power is not, therefore, built on the sentimental hope that we will all love one another. Ethical conflict is dynamic and it is sanctioned by its intention and its end. Intent, however, is not simply psychological motivation. It is objective. Ethical experience shapes intent before the fact and thus allows for a moral strategy. Conflict is judged after the fact by its outcomes and in particular by how far it has moved us along the pathway from value to worth. It is not enough, then, to claim the integrity of one's motives, to appeal to sincerity. Competence, skilled performance in the world, is at least as significant, else the connection between means and ends cannot responsibly be made.

There are morally legitimate and morally illegitimate conflicts. The ethical criteria for distinguishing them are neither mysterious nor impractical in an industrial society. The great causes, for example, are the inclusive causes, the democratic causes. Competence, moreover, is clearly more effective than instincts of "blood" or "race," or than untutored intuition. Thus, authoritarian institutions generate, sooner or later, a self-destroying resentment and in an industrial society invite covert sabotage. To be sure, some of us may still find *Gotterdämmerung* appealing in some powerful and non-rational way. But we cannot erect an ethical philosophy on such an appeal.

Actual inequalities and distinctions of power in the world of value are to be expected. Indeed, the Adler of the 1890's comes close to what we today would call a notion of "affirmative action" in his analysis of inequalities. Thus,

> The doctrine of unrestrained individualism is the doctrine of the athletes in the struggle for existence....But what chance of success will the lame man have when set on his feet...against the athlete? The inequality of conditions which is so sharply extenuated at the present day is a direct result of the doctrine of equality, for there is no surer means...of exacerbating the tendency to inequality which has always existed on account of the differences in men's natural capacities than to persuade them that such inequalities do not exist....[22]

In the world as it is and given people as they are, it is false and therefore an abuse of power to proclaim as fact "equality of opportunity" and "equality before the law." To be sure, as ends-in-view, these are worthy. But, differences of capacity, of place, of family resources and the like make these catch phrases of an unreconstructed democracy suspect and even invite cynicism.

The upshot of Adler's goal of an ethics of power is a theory of re-organization. Moved to respond to the socialist criticism of American society, Adler agrees that government by consent of the governed is not self evident nor are notions such as "that government is best that governs least" helpful in the present circumstance. In a world of large numbers and increasing specialization, representative government is surrendered in fact unless the interests of functional groups are recognized. And all of this implies a re-organization of the state, which

> alone is capable of grappling with those vast combinations...shaping them, public powers as they already are, into instruments for the public good. I believe that the government will take such action only if pressure is put upon it by the class of the population which most feels the evils of the existing system...the laboring class. And I believe especially that the laboring class can only exert such pressure by electing labor representatives to the legislatures....[23]

Conflicts of interest are inevitable in practice. But these can become morally reasonable, even progressive, only when shaped by the moral ideal. For example, no conflict may go to the point of demeaning the opponent in his or her own eyes or in those of his or her fellows. To turn the human being into the "enemy" is to deny worth to him or her. Because of the reciprocal inter-relationships of persons, this approach evokes a similar perception in the other. Under such conditions, this leaves the enemies with little recourse but a war to the death. With the ideal in mind, however, interests are understood as reaching out toward and being reached by other interests. Thus, Adler rejects socialism as "mass egotism," which is his reading of class conflict. Each in its own way, socialism and *laissez-faire* thus end with a "war of each against all." They warrant the Hobbesian conclusion that without some sovereign power, life will be "brutish, short and mean." Power without worth, however, is a *reductio ad absurdum*. Ignoring the ideal, it is left finally with nothing to control. The veto becomes absolute.

Adler turns to what he calls a "three-fold reverence" as the way of contextualizing power.

> The human race has gained a certain ethical footing in the empirical sphere....In the act of separating what is worthwhile from what is worthless...we manifest our reverence for the past. It is thus that true historicity is distinguished from blind conservatism....The second kind of reverence is directed toward those who are...approximately on the same level with us....In our relation to them we may learn the great lesson of appreciating unlikeness....The third kind of reverence is directed toward the undeveloped...the young, the backward among groups of civilized peoples and the uncivilized peoples. We are to reverence that which is potential in all of these....[24]

Adler is not foolish enough to believe that a call to reverence will be heard in the midst of battle. Yet, battles are not fought for their own sake. Regiments at war are not available to reason, but even here norms of conduct are still to be found, rules of law like the Geneva Conventions or rules of relationship like chivalry. And besides, battles have their beginnings and endings off the battle-field. Reasons are given and interests are identified, both before and after. At those points, the three-fold reverence can play its role.

Reverence is not an exhortation to virtue but a test of the adequacy or inadequacy of the reasons given and the interests identified. It appeals beyond the passions of the moment or the hidden self interest to ethical experience. In particular, it is based in the expectation that the person will recognize the other in himself or herself. Subjective to be sure as a felt response, it is yet general enough to lead to what Dewey, more modest than Adler, calls the inter-subjective.

At the same time, reverence is not an instinctive or automatic response. It is learned. For example, when Adler founded the School of Applied Ethics (1891–1895), he addressed the literacy necessary to move toward the ethical uses of power:

> it is not sufficient to explain the facts by tracing them as effects back to their causes...we must...compare them with something that lies far ahead of the facts, that is with a state of social life and modes of human conduct which have been yet been real but which ought to be real....Now this ethical side of the sciences of conduct has not heretofore been accentuated as it should have been and it is the special aim of the School of Applied Ethics to bring it into deserved prominence....[25]

Moral literacy, however, is not the achievement of any single program or institution, or of any single group or generation. It arises from self consciousness in all relationships and from realistic outcroppings of worth and radiation. We need to remember that even the worst of human beings is morally complex. "Instinct of affection moves him; he wishes to provide for wife and children...."[26] Any human activity is caught up in many human activities. Economic goals are inextricably bound up with non-economic goals; political goals with social and personal ones; *etc.* Because of this fact of experience, the reconstruction of power can enter into the life of all human beings, even into the life of the so-called villain.

That catchword of free enterprise, enlightened self interest, needs reconstruction too. It asks us to give an ethical reading of the meaning of its terms. Thus the self entails a genuine interest in personal development, and this relies on reciprocating relationships with other selves. To be enlightened is thus to be aware of the possibilities of the social self. History, indeed, directs the idea toward its institutional possibilities.

> Have you considered what good industry can do for politics?....The answer is by external organization of industry. And again, industry itself will benefit by the return effect. How can business and industry beneficently affect religion? By giving a new meaning to "laborare est orare," by so constituting work that it shall give spiritual life in the world, on the farms, in the shipyard....[27]

The unspoken assumption of Adler's reconstruction of power is that human beings want to do what is morally best and that they do not really want to violate others. These are, no doubt, rather optimistic assumptions about behavior and about the likelihood of moral knowledge. Yet, their negation would make both democracy and the human enterprise itself ethically pointless. The achievement of power would be simply silly, a confused brute strength blindly expressing itself.

Toward A Public Philosophy[28]

Unreconstructed, industrialism distorts social experience. Human beings in groups are treated as parts of a larger machine, and individuals are treated as isolates. A conceptual error is thus embedded in modern institutions and generates the gap between technical achievement and relevant symbol. Its moral outcome is the "divided conscience," the inability to deal with the public and the personal in an ethically coherent way. I know that as a member of a family or of a religious and ethnic community I am a person among persons, caring and being cared for, loving, laughing, giving. But as a member of industrial society, I am, as it were, subjected to the laws of social motion. When I hit against you, I am supposed to react as a thing and move in a determinate direction. And so too is this expected of you. We are to impact but not to connect. On this model a public ethic is reduced to mechanics, and thus appears the myth of the neutral market, the realist state, the divorce of ethics and politics, of person and society.

But ethical experience gives the lie to the inevitability of this division and to this model. I know myself differently from what I am said to be, even in the public life. The reconstruction of power, then, calls for a morality of group relationships, *i. e.,* my relationships as a member of a group to other members, my relationships to the members of other groups and most important of all the relationships of groups to each other. Failing this, I waste my energies in a power game and am afflicted by deeply felt contradictions, contradictions of identity. By the rules of an unreconstructed public life, I am to be either victor or loser and in any case a competitor against all other competitors. Yet, by the rules of family life, I live by love and personal obligation. Public and intimate life, however, are not neatly separated by absolute boundaries. The guest in my home may at the same time be the enemy of my daily activity. My child as a worker becomes a member of a group which I, as manager and owner, am fated to oppose. At the least, we also share a common citizenship and yet dare not give any depth to that citizenship. And so it goes. When to this fracturing of boundaries is added the sense of being wronged and the recognition that it is a common sense, I am even more confounded. I find myself justifying what I know to be violation, and yet that is not what I want to do, not what I know I ought to do.

Adler's project is not abstract. A felt confusion and dismay arises as I find myself morally incapacitated in the midst of others who are, like me, morally incapacitated. It is thus out of the deepest needs of intimacy that a public philosophy arises. Most dramatically, a public philosophy is a response to the need for personal tranquillity. Mystic and prophet are again joined.

Nowhere is this more clearly exhibited than in the condition of reform and the reformer. As Adler puts the matter,

> Speaking for myself, I may make this personal statement to indicate the spirit in which I approach these lectures (Plymouth, 1894), that twenty-three years ago, the reading of Frederick Albert Lange's *Arbeiter Frage* together with his critique of Mill....first kindled in me a flame of protest....since then as an ethicist, I have felt that the so-called labor question is the chief moral question of the day...all the other great moral questions and the religious questions as well must be brought into relations with this one and acquire a new depth and significance by being brought into such relations....[29]

If the mistake of the mechanistic model is left unchallenged, however, then reform is not only impractical but ethically irrelevant. Houses do not become homes, training replaces education and wage labor is confused with vocation. Adler's answer, as we know, is the metaphor of organicism, now understood as an image of institutional or educational reconstruction, a public philosophy.

Adler is not consistent, unfortunately, in his use of the terms "public" and "social." Yet, his meaning is clear enough. As a social animal, the human being has the potentiality for becoming a participant in the organic reconstruction of society. Its political vehicle is the inclusive and interdependent public. But the "public" is an ethical and not just a natural or biological idea. It connotes distinctions between public and private, raises issues of obligation, announces that the social animal has agreed to act in public, to appear before witnesses and to grant credibility to their observations, and the like. Not all social animals, however, are necessarily invited to be members of the public, *i. e.,* not all public philosophies are democratic. Putting this in another way, all human beings as such are members of society. To be invited to be a member of a public, however, is to be seen as capable of moral development in that society. And this capacity may be denied, as it has been, to women, children, people of color, immigrants, *etc.* In any case, citizenship is achieved, although historically the achievement has been tied to birth or faith or

status.   In a democratic public philosophy, however, no one is
excluded from the possibility of achieving membership.

In the transition from a traditional to a modern public, conflict
will appear, conflicting senses of what counts as a public and who shall
count for the public.   A democratic public does not come into being
without pain, not least of all the pain that arises when an inclusive
public threatens the privileges of the historic selective publics of class
or race or nationality or status.   But conflict arises not only between
future and past.   Democratic rhetoric itself masks the conflicts
embedded even in the inclusive public.

> At present under the false cloak of universal representation irrespective of
> class distinctions we have in fact the odious monopoly of governmental
> powers by one class—the wealthy class.   Let class distinctions be
> exposed to view.   Let the different classes...stand face to face with one
> another and they will not only come to terms but to a clear understanding
> of their mutual interdependence....[30]

Ultimately, these historic and modern conflicts are to be resolved
by solving the problem of the divided conscience, by getting to the
root of the matter which is the gulf between inconsistent public and
private moralities.   Thus, the American may well be politically
democratic, economically autocratic, communally cooperative and
socially competitive all at once.   And that is both psychologically and
morally intolerable.   For Adler, organicism is the key.   Under its
inspiration, the self is the social self; intimacy is also a form of
sociability.   No metaphysical barrier stands between public and private
worlds.   On organic grounds, they create each other.   So the human
being is not trapped in dualism with the soul in one world and the role
in another.   Tensions of course will always arise and sometimes they
will be located in conflict between the needs of intimacy and the needs
of sociability.   This is a sign that value has not entirely been replaced
by worth, that the spiritual manifold remains ideal.   But these tensions
are no longer the irreparable cosmological conflicts brought on by
membership in disparate worlds.

> A man engaged in large business transactions approached a Christian
> clergyman of my acquaintance with this request: "Can you tell me how I
> can lead a Christian life in business?" and the clergyman confided to me
> that he had found it difficult to give a satisfactory answer.   Difficulty, I
> reflected, on Christian premises, is it possible?[31]

Adler's term for the conduct that unites the intimate and the public is "service," and in particular social service in the public arena. Generically, service is the mode of doing for another and, typically, thereby doing for oneself as well. It begins in the love of parents for each other and for their children and matures in the relationships of friend to friend, the acts of vocation, and the duties of citizenship. Service becomes the active form of the public over time; the way we are to conduct ourselves in public. Moreover, it is learned since competence in service builds on prior service. It follows that the way the public is constituted determines the kinds of things that are taught and learned. A democratic public teaches one kind of lesson, an autocratic public, another. As it were, we all begin with what is nearest and manageable. As we mature and if we are regarded as eligible, we learn to be more competent, to enlarge and then again enlarge the arena of social action. Adler's model remains evolutionary and developmental.

> When parents began to sacrifice for their children, then the ethicizing began; then the law of the jungle was overcome. For the law of the jungle is life at the expense of life and the ethical law is life in promoting life. And so, in a similar way, we shall begin the ethicizing of nations...creating and fostering the best development according to their own needs.[32]

The world of an unreconstructed industrialism lacks a sense of public service just because it lacks a sense of the other as person. Under free market inspiration, all of us are private warriors. The rules we follow are merely traffic rules, or rules of the game. Neither justice nor obligation but prudence is the guiding principle. Under such a condition, the self does not develop and reform cannot succeed. As Robert Guttchen remarks, "Justice assumes a public world...[but] the modern demand for a group ethic is made in the context in which no public world is recognized....We may read the demand, in effect, as the demand...to build such a world."[33] Trying to avoid this bleak conclusion, the free market pretends to stop at the factory door, the office door, the tradesman's door. Patriotic rhetoric and family ties are still celebrated. But the market invades the personal space, and the personal space tries to return the favor. Since these appear as contradictory realities, however, the invasion is felt as aggression and efforts at conquest, in other words, as a state of war. A public philosophy, by contrast, directs the potential citizen of the potential public, a public yet to be achieved, to the need for present

activity.   It sets the direction and context for the political and
economic reconstruction of conduct.

The Use and Abuse of the State

The institutional expression of the public is the state itself. The
state, then, is ethically necessary. Thus Adler rejects Lenin's notion of
the "withering away of the state."   He dismisses, too, the anarchist
who views the state as inherently evil and the free marketeer who views
that state as a "necessary evil."   The state has legitimate and
indispensable roles to play and not the least of these are moral. It is
the guarantor of fairness, of justice, as much as it is the agent of
administration. It also has affirmative moral responsibilities,

> It follows...that the State representing society as a whole should not
> undertake the functions, for instance, of the family, should not attempt to
> educate children in public nurseries and also that the State should not
> attempt to discharge the functions of the various vocations....The
> statement just made, however, needs to be qualified....It does not exhaust
> the conception of a superior social organism to say that its duty is merely
> the negative one of respecting the independence of its sub-
> organisms....[Its] function is to provide the common conditions for the
> best possible discharge of their proper function by all the several
> organs....[34]

As with any organism, the state also develops.   Its *telos* in a
reconstructed industrial society is to create and insure the conditions
of freedom, to allow for the exercise of distinctiveness, to enable
people to serve. Thus, Adler, as against what we call the "watchman
state" provides for "public luxuries" like museums, parks, beautiful
buildings, the arts and sculpture. These are neither "frills" nor
illegitimate undertakings. The state is not merely utilitarian.[35] Adler
adds that so-called luxuries have their economic value too and so are
not to be taken as mere expenditures.

> There are two practical ways in which we can improve the conditions of
> wage earners. The one is by increasing wages....The other way is to place
> material and intellectual goods within their reach freely and without
> price....Where a public library exists in any town, it is the same as if so
> many dollars had been added to the pay of each working man in that
> town....Public parks, public baths, the reduction of fares on street
> railways, and the like all belong in the same category....Where access is
> granted without money, provided the conditions under which it is granted

are not pauperizing and degrading, there exists what we may call virtual income, or better, virtual property....[36]

Adler's idea of service, the way in which we are to behave as members of the public, is the social worker's ideal cleared of paternalism or condescension. On this ground, the state is subject to moral judgment. Are those served, for example, taken as objects of charity or as participating citizens who also serve in different ways? In the democratic state, everyone serves and everyone is served. That is the intention of the state as an organized, an organicized, public.

There are, to be sure, distinctions of competence. Service then will be individuated, distinctive. In a democratic state, however, an invidious distinction between clients and citizens is impermissible. Of course, some of us some of the time will be beneficiaries only or primarily. We may, for example, be sick or helpless. But ultimately, the state is obliged to make room for service and to teach the capacity for service to all of its citizens.

The service ideal awaits reconstruction, but it is simultaneously its active agent in the public life. Adler tries to avoid the mistake of the reformer who, having won the vote or secured the money assumes that, with this or that project, reform is achieved. At the same time, Adler's pacing, his sense of history and the "three-fold reverence," his reliance on a developmental or evolutionary model betray a conservative temperament inconsistent with his own public actions. It is possible, for example, for the state to make sudden as well as gradual changes, and indeed usually it does both at the same time. Adler's work on the Tenement House Commission, his support of Henry George for New York mayor and his membership in what became the City Club must surely have taught him that. The "Americanization" of immigrant populations came relatively rapidly, over a generation or two, as social institutions like the police and fire departments and the political club house became vehicles for social and personal mobility.

Adler insists, however, that an organism cannot be hurried and that to do so is to insure failure or to invite illusion, the failure and illusion of the reformers who cannot understand why their successes do not produce results and why it seems that, like Sisyphus, we must climb the mountain again and again. His metaphors remain those of nurture, cultivation, individuation and, finally, time.

The organized state is not, for Adler, the activist state. It cannot do everything morally necessary, nor should it try. But, it does have a duty to the common conditions of growth. It is not only to set standards for necessities like a living wage and decent housing, but to attend as well to how these are provided. Again, charity is to give way to participation, *noblesse oblige* to democracy, as in the participatory ideology of the early settlement house movement. The state is morally legitimate only as it fulfills its moral obligations in a moral way. Of course, the public philosophy is, like any ideal, never finally achievable. Any state is transitional. So the political question to be asked is about its direction and its purpose. Again, Adler turns to the personal life to make a public point. For example,

> under the new theory of equality of women—though it is destined to produce in the end a higher type of conjugal relation—[we are] led at first to disastrous results....The moral force that could turn to account the doctrine of equality of the sexes in order to create a new type of marital relation is not yet sufficiently developed....Hence the poignancy and bitterness with which the question is asked, "Is marriage a failure?"...And modern marriage is a failure among those who stand between the old and the new, who have lost the selfish motive...and have not yet grown into the larger and unselfish spirit....[37]

Impatience leads to solutions that are non-solutions. More dangerous morally is the fact that impatience may easily lead to the total state which is, on Adler's view, an implication of socialism. It is not the philosophic materialism of Marx that most troubles Adler as much as the uses to which it is put. "[Socialism] trusts the environment to change human nature." With that externalization of responsibility, with the failure to recognize the personal and the interactive, the door is opened to intrusion by the collective into the inviolable, and to moral abdication by the individual. Moreover, the democratic state needs the corrective presences of distinctiveness, of varied persons and of varied groups. Adler sees the state as an ethical necessity, but in a non-ideal world countervailing forces are needed as well. Nurture needs resistance and tension. Moreover, in a world still governed by value, pluralism is both a practical and moral requirement. For example, "Private property," Adler writes, "is the loophole through which invention escapes into the world."[38]

The public interest, the state's program, cannot be neglected, and it too can develop toward the ideal. But the personal interest and even the partial and hardly formed interests of groups provide energy, ethical energy. Difference and differentiation, again organic metaphors, make this possible. By contrast, a monolithic philosophy—and that is how Adler reads both the private world of *laissez-faire* and the public world socialism—is mechanistic and simplistic. Instead, "The system I have in view involves individual ownership and collective use...."[39]

In developing his view of the state, the mood of advocacy that always appears in Adler's style often sets his opponents up as convenient targets. The reformers, the free marketeers, the socialists become foils for his ethical criticism and his goal of reconstruction. He gives them a less charitable reading than he does his religious and traditional opponents. No doubt, this follows from his sense that they are fellow members of the reform neighborhood, actual competitors in the process of reconstruction. Traditional religion, on the other hand, is the historic occasion of an earlier time that still lingers on as an echo of the past. Thus he misses or underplays the ethical motives that animate the passion of the reformer, the basis of socialism, the hopefulness of the free market. Nevertheless, Adler's realistic sense of the limits of reform and of the dangers of an allegedly non-moral political economy from right or left remain relevant. Thus Adler warns against the totalitarian impulse and the morally debilitating consequences of charity for both giver and receiver. Adler's vocabulary calls attention to tempo and interdependence. Thus, too, he points to the necessity and limits of conflict. The dialectic of the democratic state, finally, arises from the tension embedded in the three-fold reverence, the notion that we in the present both cannot and yet continually try to escape the past and embrace the future. We never quite make it, but we never quite fall back unchanged.

Spiritual Democracy

The climactic theme of Adler's reconstruction of power is spiritual democracy. Inclusiveness, inter-relationship and participation are the embedded potency of an industrial society. For a spiritual democracy these appear, ideally, as the emergence of each personality through the talents, the inclusion of each person in an orchestration of persons and the evolution of work from mechanism toward productivity. Education, practically and ideally, is the process of realization. Thus, candidates for office, political parties and government officials are derivative and not primary in Adler's politics. Power and culture connect. Individuals, laws, and public actions are the occasions of that connection. Education and politics are its process.

The signs of a state that is in the process of reconstruction are to be found in the maturing ability of individuals to contribute to the public good and the maturing ability of society to welcome the contribution. Above all, however, Adler does not forget the reciprocal

development of self and self. Social duty always has its personal
sanction.

Social reform is the reformation of all the social institutions in such a
way that they may become successive phrases through which the
individual shall advance toward the acquisition of an ethical
personality....[40]

By identifying citizenship with development, Adler avoids
democratic formalism. Democracy, with its emphasis on political and
legal procedures, is easily vulnerable to being reduced to political
structures. Spiritual democracy is substantive and its issue is the
distribution of power throughout a competent population. But power,
as we have seen, is not simply a matter of choosing who shall and who
shall not rule by means of elections nor even of referendums. Adler's
pluralism, the necessity of countervailing competence groups, relies
on inalienable power. Election, then, is not a periodic transfer
between or among ruler and ruled but a continuing directive under
conditions of on-going and popular judgment. The political life of
the state is a continuous ebb and flow and not a set of dramatic
moments when things change one way or another. It is doubtful, thus,
that "checks and balances" and extended terms of office can serve
Adler's purpose. He is more likely an advocate of parliamentarianism
with its uninterrupted connection between act and response. The
organic image, by and large, calls for continuities and not
periodicities. Toward the end of his life, Adler even raises questions
about his idea of the vocational reconstruction of the state. It is, he
says, an "over simplification"[41] and is still wedded to an agrarian
model of representation.

Solving the problems of the divided conscience in practice is
intended by Adler's reconstruction of citizenship to be
simultaneously personal and public. Adler has in mind clichéd
references to Sunday and weekday morality, conflicts between
personal integrity and political opportunism, the irrelevance of
religious values to society. But it is not enough to rely on generalities.
A young man when the scandals of the Grant administration were in
the public eye, and alive to the emerging era of bossism and the
smoke-filled room, Adler knows first hand the corruptions of
democratic citizenship. Hence, his concern with the rights of children,
of women, of labor as conditions of inclusion and participation.
Without these rights, inclusion is impossible and participation
incompetent. A spiritual democracy is then only utopian. Rights are
not merely boundary conditions, conditions of non-violation. For

Adler, they have an affirmative and active intention as well, in brief, an educational intention. Thus, rights are forms of power. For example, Adler writes,

> on what plea of justice can we deny (women) admission to higher grades
> of service...to open all the professions to their entrance, to open all the
> professional schools (to) them....Is not the demand for higher culture
> equally necessary for [wives and mothers]?...[They] should be able to pass
> an intelligent judgment upon the political issues of the day...should
> possess sufficient familiarity with the natural sciences to understand at
> least the results...to gain some knowledge of the human body...[of]
> whatever pertains to the education of young children....[42]

Adler's theory of work is his attempt to answer the problem of representation and so, ultimately, of equity as well. But economic justice cannot simply wait on the future, nor is it only a question of a living wage. Simply to pay attention to this reform or that reform, to wages and hours, for example, is to ignore the move toward the ideal. It is also to ignore the question of how to live a good life, or as good a life as possible, in a market place society.

Adler's imagination moves freely between ideal and real, present and future and, admittedly, this sometimes jeopardizes the consistency of his philosophic ideas. But his seeming asides—as in his more topical Sunday addresses—are often initial responses to ethical experience and after reflection stimulate a reconsideration of the ideal. Thus, his educational and his political philosophy remain unfinished. For example, as we have seen when he suggests a kind of proto affirmative action policy in reflecting on equality, he also envisions an automated society in reflecting on productivity.

> It is conceivable also that a time may come when automatic machinery
> will to a much larger extent than now take the place of human labor and
> the energy required for the production of commodities will be reduced to a
> minimum. When this utopian condition shall have been reached, it may
> be safe for government to undertake the general management of
> industries....At that time, however, the need of education through
> vocation would not disappear....If industrial activity should be reduced to
> a minimum, new vocations would doubtless arise....[43]

Work, in other words, is not only an economic activity, and productivity is a capacity of the human being as such. The emergence of new vocations is a feature of reconstruction and is for

us a commonplace. But it was already visible for Adler in the move
from farm to factory, from town to city.

Adler says little if anything about leisure. I suspect, however, that
he would reconstruct it as well. For example, productivity implies
doing that which produces not simply objects but personal
distinctiveness. Leisure, then, would be judged by its developmental
effects. Moreover, the objects of productivity are, unlike those of
wage labor, outcomes of personality. So craftsmanship and art
suggest the directions Adler might have taken. In any event, it is clear
enough that merely killing time would not do. Adler had evidence
enough of self-destroying trivialities in the history of the *ancien
regime* and in that of the new aristocrats, the success stories of an
unreconstructed market place.

Spiritual democracy requires life-long learning. In childhood,
the family is the school. But in a differentiated industrial society,
sophistication and specialization are unavoidable, and this is as true of
the school and the family as of the workplace. New relationships are
always in the making. For example,

> Home and school should not merely cooperate but interpenetrate....The
> school is to prepare its charges not only for vocational life but for
> citizenship. Teachers...must keep in living contact with the civic and
> social movements of the time...[and show] reverence for the undeveloped
> human being...its latent personality....We show our reverence for the
> child in the effort to personalize it.[44]

Adler's philosophy is, at every point, a philosophy of
reconstructing institutions, relying on the capacity of persons to make
that happen. He consistently sets out to test his ideas in practice. For
example, The Ethical Culture Schools are to have a political *telos*.
"The ideal of the School is not the adaptation of the individual to the
existing social environment; it is to develop persons who will be
competent to change their environment...that is, to put it boldly, to
train reformers...."[45] The climactic effort in this direction is Adler's
proposal for a "pre-vocational school for business, " the Fieldston
plan, where the children of labor and of management would teach and
reach each other, and not just learn skills and subject matters.

> I will ask him [the business man] to let me have his son....I have at the
> back of my head the idea of a school of commerce...which shall be two
> things...[Its students] must be efficient as any of the graduates of the best
> business schools. We want no sloppy work...in addition, we want men
> who are progressive...in and through business attaining culture....the

youth I am going to educate...[is] to get the feeling of solidarity with mankind....[46]

Just as home and school are to interpenetrate, so students are also to be participants, active and not simply passive. They are to help each other just as they are to take part in governance.[47] Teachers and students are not set apart from each other as distinct classes. All the members of the school, parents, teachers and students, are to be masters to some and apprentices to others. Of course, the teacher knows more than the student about many things. But he or she also knows less, as well. Reciprocity is the key here too, the key to curriculum development, if you will. Functional groups will develop as organized bodies of students, teachers and parents. Individuality and not category is the essential point. Thus, in another echo of progressivism, the school both is and models spiritual democracy.

No doubt, there will be conflicts in such a school just as there are conflicts in society. But these are means of education and not occasions for arbitrary rule and repression. What sustains the process is a common interest. In practice, however, that common interest is also an educational assignment: it must be discovered and developed, not just given. The theme is "becoming a person," but that is only form. The school at any moment and with its particular group of parents teachers and students, is, as it were, an occasion for giving the form its content. Schooling is thus preparatory for the larger work of social reconstruction.

Adler's practical efforts are devoted to elementary and secondary education. But, he is not unfamiliar with the university. Although a minor note in his philosophy of education, he notes that

[a] university is a group of vocational schools. A truly democratic university is an organic system...which in the relations that subsist between its schools affords a shining stimulating example of the kind of relations that ought to subsist between the vocational groups in the state....

The aim of an American university should be to furnish leaders for all the various groups who will undertake the great business of truly organizing democracy.[48]

There is an Emersonian flavor to Adler's Americanization of the university. It is to be, if you will, the "American Scholar" institutionalized.

Finally, the continuing educational institution is the vocation itself. Adler is more than familiar with the nascent labor movement, with Thomas Davidson's Breadwinner's College and, above all, with the on-going work of the settlement house. In these various efforts, as with the Summer School of Applied Ethics, the aim is political. The momentary interest, the hobby or fad, is not really adult education at all. "A mature person who is deficient in theoretical education needs to be helped to interpret his vocational experience...." And, of course, that interpretation is shaped by culture and *telos*. As a mode of evolving competence, it enables the person to participate more effectively in an organized democracy.

In his brief and sporadic references to the university and adult education, Adler reveals his priorities. The child, the young and the family are at the top. The rest, he almost seems to say, will follow when and as these are attended to. But he also reveals his assumptions. Thus, he attends much more carefully to the education of women than to the education of men, as in the Women's Society for the Study of Child Nature, and much more carefully to the specialty than to the citizen in general, as in the Businessman's Group. Development, in other words, is not a generalized process but relies on the moment, the specialty and the need. The lessons of ethical experience are to be used to produce powerful persons and those lessons teach of distinctiveness, individuality, specialty and connection. Spiritual democracy is not an exhortation and not a form but an action.

Notes

[1] Felix Adler, "The Spiritual Basis of Reconstruction," address, January 5, 1919, p. 1

[2] Felix Adler, "The New Education: Its Triumphs and Defects," address, April 29, 1900, pp. 18-20.

[3] Felix Adler, "The Foundation of a Better Social Order as Laid in Education," address, January 29, 1922, p. 6

[4] Adler, "Twelfth Lecture," Plymouth, p. 8.

[5] Adler, "First Lecture on Culture", Oxford, pp. 6-7.

[6] For a discussion of Adler's political record, see Howard B. Radest, *Common Ground:* the Republican Convention, p. 41, Henry George and the New York City mayoralty campaigns, pp. 41 and 176, the "Committee of 15" and the election of a reform administration, pp. 128 and 176.

[7] Adler, *Religion of Duty*, pp. 67-68.

[8] Adler, *An Ethical Philosophy*, pp. 260-261.

[9] Adler, "Twelfth Lecture," Plymouth, p. 3.

[10] For a description of Adler's views on imperialism, racism and chauvinism in America, see Radest, *Common Ground*, Chapter XV, pp. 165-177.

[11] Adler, "The Foundation of a Better Social Order," p. 16.

[12] Felix Adler, "American Ideals Contrasted With German and English," address, undated but probably 1914-1915, p. 5.

[13] Adler, "American Ideals," p. 5.

[14] Felix Adler, *The Essentials of Spirituality*, New York, James Pott and Co., 1905, pp. 35-45.

[15] Felix Adler, *The Moral Instruction of Children*, New York, D. Appleton and Co., 1898, p. 243.

[16] Adler was not opposed to the use of force. In an essay, "The Exercise of Force in the Interest of Freedom" (*An Ethical Philosophy*, pp. 369-372), he describes the conditions that justify coercion by the state: "....stimulative and repressive social coercions are justified in so far as they provoke energy and check disturbing impulses." He adds, "A given society is apt to mistake its prejudice for principle....Yet, on the whole the benefits of coercion outweigh the detriments." The revolutionary would therefore have to defend the use of force for the sake of the ideal. Perhaps, this could be justified in a totalitarian state, in a military dictatorship or against colonial conquest. Revolution is to be rare and situational.

[17] Felix Adler, *Minutes*, Board of Trustees, New York Society for Ethical Culture, February 5, 1917.

[18] Guttchen, *Felix Adler's Ethics*, pp. 36-37.

[19] Adler, *Reconstruction*, pp. 71-72.

[20] Felix Adler, "Faust's Salvation or Goethe's Doctrine of Salvation," address, November 26, 1905, pp. 2-3.

[21] Adler, *Essentials of Spirituality*, pp. 68-69.

[22] Adler, "Eighth Lecture," Plymouth, pp. 14-15.

[23] Adler, "Fourth Lecture," Plymouth, pp. 7-8.

[24] Adler, *An Ethical Philosophy*, pp. 244-245.

[25] Felix Adler, "Opening Exercises of the School of Applied Ethics," 1894, pp. 7-8.

[26] Adler, "Second Lecture," Plymouth, p. 7.

[27] Adler, "Second Lecture," Plymouth, p. 7.

[28] Obviously, this title owes its debt to Walter Lippman. Thus, Lippman wrote,

> The crucial point, however, is not where the naturalists and supernaturalists disagreed. It is that they did agree that there was a valid law which, whether it was the commandment of God or the reason of things, was transcendent. They did agree that it was not something decided upon by certain men and then proclaimed by them. It was not someone's fancy, someone's prejudice, someone's wish or rationalization, a psychological experience and no more....It can be discovered. It has to be obeyed.

Adler, of course, recognized the public claim on the private and the private claim on the public. These were ethically objective and not reducible to psychology or to physics. Citation is from *The Essential Lippmann*, Clinton Rossiter and James Lare, editors, New York, Random House, 1963, pp. 200–201.

[29] Adler, "First Lecture," Plymouth, p. 2–3.

[30] Adler, "Eleventh Lecture," Plymouth, p. 17.

[31] Adler, *Reconstruction*, p. 25n.

[32] Felix Adler, "The Ideal Society of Nations," address, April 30, 1916, p. 17.

[33] Guttchen, *Felix Adler's Ethics*, p. 24.

[34] Adler, "Eleventh Lecture," Plymouth, pp. 2–4.

[35] Adler, "Eleventh Lecture," Plymouth, pp. 13–14.

[36] Adler, "Fourth Lecture," Plymouth, pp. 3–4.

[37] Adler, "Fifth Lecture," Plymouth, pp. 8–9.

[38] Adler, "Sixth Lecture," Plymouth, p. 5.

[39] Adler, "Sixth Lecture," Plymouth, p. 5.

[40] Adler, *An Ethical Philosophy*, p. 261.

[41] This comment was recalled by Horace Friess in a conversation. The further development of Adler's vocationalism was, Friess thought, very much on Adler's mind at the last seminar he attended in 1932. Sadly, he never did have time to follow up on this concern.

[42] Felix Adler, "The Education of Women to Freedom," address, April 22, 1877, pp. 7–13.

[43] Adler, "Eleventh Lecture," Plymouth, pp. 10–11.

[44] Adler, *An Ethical Philosophy*, p. 295.

[45] Felix Adler, "The Distinctive Aims of the Ethical Culture School," address, undated (probably some time between 1915 and 1920), pp. 4–5

[46] Felix Adler, "Is Culture Compatible with Democracy?" address, January 27, 1924, pp. 7–9.

[47] Before the Fieldston plan was fully worked out, Adler was well along in moving from the experience of building the Schools to their meaning for development and democracy. In fact, he had already identified the importance of "student councils" in the Plymouth lecture in 1894. As he sums it up,

A vital system of self government is to be used as a means of placing real responsibility upon the students...The more gifted pupils of the schools should be invited to take a personal interest in helping the more backward students...there are...shy, sensitive, solitary youths...the task of bring them into fellowship offers one of the finest opportunities for ethical education....

Adler, *An Ethical Philosophy*, p. 304n.
[48] Adler, *An Ethical Philosophy*, pp. 300–301.

VI

INSIGHT OR ILLUSION

Reprise

Felix Adler is ordinarily referred to as the founder of a non-conforming religious movement or of a progressive school. His philosophy, however, is remembered, if at all, as but a minor instance of post-Kantian idealism.[1] On reflection, the dismissal is understandable but misguided. Adler is indeed a religious innovator, an insightful commentator and critic of politics, economics and education. He is an institution builder as well. But, these disparate efforts are grounded in an emerging philosophy that marries Kantian idealism with pragmatism and romanticism. In turn, his philosophy is shaped by his experience as a reformer. Idealism and practicalism thus nourish each other. Moreover, Adler is seized by substantive ethical issues of his time and many of these are still problematic today. He still speaks to the present. His concerns and responses, however, are never simply topical. Above all, it is ethical experience seen from the perspective of an inventive philosophic mind that serves as the bridge between idea and action.

The Socratic question still lives for all of us: is an ethical life possible, and, if so, how is it to be achieved? This is *the* question that shapes Adler's vocation. Attentive to what he calls the historic occasion, he restates the question concretely: is an ethical life possible under the conditions of a commercial and technologically sophisticated society? In other words, how can a mass culture and an industrial society be genuinely democratic? Questions of power and practice inevitably follow. In short, Adler is both of his time and of our own in identifying the moral dilemmas and possibilities of the modern world.

Ironically, Adler's effectiveness in the varied roles he plays over a long and busy life-time tend to mask his originality. Politicians can dismiss him as only a reformer, reformers, as only a philosopher and philosophers, as only a preacher. Then, too, his dominant role in a small and marginal movement often insulates him from criticism. For the members of the Ethical Societies, Adler is, after all, "the founder!" Of course, his Columbia University colleagues did not hesitate to voice their doubts and disagreements. As an idealist—or at least as someone who uses an idealist vocabulary—he is simply out of step with their naturalism and, more generally, with the evolving linguistic and positivistic temper of Anglo-American ethical philosophy.

Adler's style is adapted to the public platform, and his written work betrays its rhetorical roots. Yet, even in popular discourse, he clearly demonstrates that his convictions arise from the ideas of a skeptical intelligence and a critical temperament. He is, to be sure, always the preacher. But, while preaching adds an element of passion, it does not blind him to the complexities of experience and the need for disciplined reflection nor does he see the world in the black and white of moralism.

Adler's neo-Kantian rigor is embedded in an existential mood. For all the rationalism of his philosophic sources, he is sensitive to despair and even to absurdity. Thus his sharp distinction between value and worth is both an analytic tool and a commentary on the need to transcend self-righteous judgment. Again and again, Adler returns to the theme of the pains of experience, the divided conscience, failure and frustration. And it is clear enough that these themes are not just categories and modes of perception but of personal feeling.

There is nearly always an autobiographical quality in Adler's utterance. For example,

> We are living in a curious age....the most noticeable thing about the *Zeitgeist* is the reaction in favor of some kind of belief....it is due to the unrest of modern life, to the disillusionment with the pursuit of pleasure....Those who have got (wealth) see that...the game is not worth the candle....another cause is the failure of physical science to offer a substitute for religion as it was one time expected to do....another cause is the postponement of the social millennium...a combination of longing and hopelessness....[2]

Many of Adler's insights have stood the test of experience.[3] Yet he has been nearly forgotten. Even in Ethical Culture, *his* movement, Adler's thought is neglected in favor of a certain piety toward an admittedly charismatic figure. No doubt his location in a moment of cultural, political and philosophical transition also invites a certain obscurity. After all, he is never only of one kind of place or time. His life spans the period from the Civil War to the rise of Hitler. His New York City *milieu*—upper middle class, Jewish[4] and cosmopolitan—is ambiguously European and American. Often traditional in his symbols, Adler's references are classic and contemporary. European in his philosophic *genre*, his problems are peculiarly American. Unfortunately, he has many followers but few critics.

Adler certainly begins as a Kantian.[5] But he is also a progressive, and he is nourished by the Americanism of Jefferson, Lincoln and Emerson. He is not a little bit of a romantic and surely a pragmatist. Given his practicalism, he is as much a situationalist as an essentialist in ethics. Surely, his attention to detail, to individuation, to difference forces him over and over again to confess that principle does not seem to cover the case and reason does not resolve its problems. But he does not then surrender to the situation, rich as it is in its detail and in its uniqueness. Thus, the distinction between value and worth is his attempt to achieve coherence in the face of the elusiveness of ethical experience.

Adler may well be faulted for a certain looseness of style. For the preacher, careful argument is often surrendered to the striking phrase and the ear-catching illustration. Even if this predilection were muted, his themes remain embedded in events and, as such, are never neatly available without over-simplification. Thus, it is well to recall Aristotle's advice.

> Our discussion will be adequate if it has as much clearness as the subject-matter admits of, for precision is not to be sought for alike in all discussions any more than in all the products of the crafts...We must be content, then, in speaking of such subjects...to indicate the truth roughly...for it is the mark of an educated man to look for precision in each class of things just so far as the nature of the subject admits....[6]

If you will, Adler's philosophy is appropriately metaphoric, even at times, a kind of philosophic poetry.

Adler surely engages in polemic and he is, in turn, the object of attack from traditionalists in religion, education and politics. Yet, he probes beneath institution, action and person for continuing and deeper meanings. Difference, for him, is generative and so demands respect. For example, unlike nineteenth century atheists and free thinkers, he is not often given to taking the cudgels to supernaturalism. His critique of Christianity for its lack of a relevant ethic and of Judaism for its tribalism is not the polemic of the religious radical. He remains in hope of reconstruction everywhere. John Herman Randall, Jr. suggests the context of Adler's spiritual problem, the deliberate abdication of traditional religions, their failure to meet the moral needs of persons in the market place.

The most revolutionary change introduced by the great Protestant reformers into the medieval scheme of salvation was...to make the moral life and its social repercussions something human and independent....Salvation must precede conduct as the indispensable condition of the moral life. As the reformers put it, salvation comes from religious faith not from moral good works....[7]

Even when Adler deals with issues like the exploitation of labor, the rights of women or the abuse of children, it is the religious philosopher and not just the reformer who speaks. He is troubled by a tradition that ignores these things because it rationalizes moral passivity in theology, rite and conduct. He does his work, after all, before the "social gospel" appears and before tradition's discovery of the "secular city." His is a philosophy of religious protest, but it is a philosophy and not just an extended editorial.

Worth And The Moral Imagination

Like a ghost, the idea of worth haunts Adler. There it is, impossible to dispense with and yet, in the face of ethical experience, difficult to hold on to. Above all, Adler, ever the realist, wants to build an ethics of reconstruction. The starting point is human conduct as it shows itself in the historic occasion. As such, it cannot be dismissed. Human beings and the human situation are just too mixed and changeable for an ethics of pure principle. Thus, we have Adler's effort to work out an evolutionary relationship between "is" and "ought." He is honest enough to confess that he attributes worth but does not find it in persons. Ultimately, it is a programmatic and not a cosmological notion. As he says, over and over again and in many different ways, worth is to be verified by the future even if it has its outcroppings in the present. The idea of worth does double duty. It sounds a warning when we are tempted to go too far, a temptation typical of the technicist mind. It is thus addressed to the activist and to the reformer as much as to the exploiter. A practical interest in consequences, positive and negative, is worth's ground but these consequences are in themselves moral outcomes and quite different from the market place's bottom line.

Worth, for Adler, is traced to eighteenth century natural rights philosophy, although he embeds it in the American mission, and not in a universal declaration or in a state of nature. Like all his ideas, worth is put to work, as in his argument with the social sciences and psychiatry for crossing the boundaries of intimacy. With worth as his instrument, he also criticizes the progressives in education as "provisionalists" who lack a reliable end in view and so confuse change with direction. And it is on the grounds of worth that he challenges Kantianism itself as formalistic and abstract.

In language reminiscent of Dewey's notion of "funded experience," Adler names his source,

> there remains as a residue a common deposit of moral truth, a common stock of moral judgments, which we may call a common conscience. It is upon this common conscience that we build.[8]

Adler's reliance on history is perhaps stronger than his faith in rationality.

Intuition and feeling play their role in Adler's thought. He is a man of deep passions. Although, always the proper Victorian gentleman, these passions are deliberately kept hidden in his public appearance. He has, in short a public and a private face. Yet, there are times when he shows himself.

> Life to me is a task. It is shot through with deep anticipations of distant future joy, but on the whole it is a serious, often a desperately heavy task....I think of life as of a ...moral struggle....Life to me, even the life of the best, is always checkered, a motley web of good and evil....[9]

And in a similar comment, he later writes,

> What does it all mean and what do I mean in the scheme of things....The key...is in my own bosom. Philosophers have tried in vain...constructing a metaphysical picture of the world and then finding a place for man in it. I find a way out of my own perplexities...by searching for a point where the infinite appears in human nature itself, enveloping my spiritual nature with the infinite company of spiritual beings related to it....[10]

Worth grounds the preacher's authority, the teacher's vocation and the critic's reflection. Thus, worth has many faces and is used in different but related ways to shape Adler's project. Its complex functions are situated in the human being's autobiography as a distinctive rational and social being. But, the moral truth of the matter is never merely my truth, never merely subjective. The puzzle of its objectivity, however, justifies Adler's doubt about the way Enlightenment reason has shaped the inviolability and autonomy of the person as abstracted universals, forms without content. Experience, after all, reveals the dispensability of creatures that are supposed to be indispensable. Everyone is touched by sin, by failure, by frustration. Reason's reliance on the universal thus defeats reason itself. It points to the need to transcend experience for the sake of experience and to transcend reason for the sake of reason. For too many idealists, however, reason ends by rejecting experience. Adler, therefore, brings the sacred, now secularized, down to earth to save reason. Worth is thus a postulate prior to experience, an inference from experience and a hope for experience.

The Kantian inspiration remains. The distinctions between value and worth and between empirical and ideal are rooted in the distinction between phenomenal and noumenal. But Adler does not elevate the distinction to ontological status, nor does he, like Hegel, look for the realization of the idea in history. Instead, in his hands, the distinction turns heuristic. The possibility of reconstruction presumes that human beings are capable of imagining the end and the means, that they have the capability of seeing into the future, as it were. Adler's *a priori* is active in the world and not noetic.

Adler deliberately rejects the language of the "sacred." But, the language of worth is as problematic. So Adler still chooses not to give a neutral name to the untouchable, to that which sets a limit to activity and to intellect. Worth, after all, has its emotional and historic connotations too. For some, it is mere sentimentality. For others, it carries the weight of tradition. And for still others, it demands an act of faith. None of this is to be ignored as he makes clear in discussing the "three-fold reverence." Indeed, reconstruction requires moral literacy and reverence toward the past as toward the future. Thus, Adler captures the familiar in unfamiliar ways. In fact, worth is for him a philosophic and pedagogic strategy.

Worth is not a property but a term of sociality, a term of moral anthropology. Achieving distinctiveness of identity defines its activity. In that way, Adler differentiates his idea of worth from the soul-stuff of Christianity, the "over-soul" of Emerson and the "substance" of Spinoza. Adler's spiritual pluralism, participation in the infinite manifold, is the soul's project. Pluralism, then, is not in the first instance a political idea and certainly not a mere accommodation to the facts of American demography. Pluralism identifies the problem of a coherent universe. In such a universe, a rational being would play his or her own part in the world. Each member would thus be responsible for making a unique contribution, and the world would have to be one that accepted contribution. Failing that, the rationality of the rational being would be pointless. More than a single rational being would be redundant and a world which included multiplicity without purpose would be incoherent.

Identity, then, is not a psychological or cultural fact but an ethical necessity. To be known is to be known in particular; to act is to act in particular.

But Adler is never quite the rationalist, and so he never quite comes to terms with the ontological status of his ideas, and he knows it. Attribution and axiology are hardly adequate to a situation dominated by the opportunistic empiricism of an industrial society. So it is not surprising that, at times, Adler seems to claim that *logos* is implicit in *cosmos,* as in his reference to the supersensible and his evident confidence in the ultimate reasonableness of the universe. But he does not often take this path and certainly never comfortably. Pressed, he calls these views his faith. More often than not, however, he is content with an instrumental approach to concepts and hesitates to claim more for the ideal as such than that it serves as an end in view, a direction, almost as an aesthetic notion, a creation of the moral imagination.

A rational and social being requires a certain kind of reality in order to be rational and sociable, and for better or worse we are rational and social. A world that has no place for what makes its creatures what they are would be an insane world, an absurdity. Thus far, Adler is willing to go in assigning existence to worth and the infinite manifold. But he stops short of cosmology,

> Not the realization of the ideal is our earthly goal, but the realization of the reality of the ideal. To the rational nature, only the rational can be real. The data of sense are real to us so far as they are rationalized. They can never wholly be rationalized. There always remains an irreducible residuum of the irrational....[11]

Again, it is the moral imagination at work. As it were, Adler asks his reader to conceive a world that is incoherent. It would, of necessity, be a world without society, *i. e.,* a world where relationships were arbitrary, momentary and unreliable. In such a world, the human being would experience the frustration of unrelieved and unrelievable purposelessness. And even dubious purposes like profit and conquest could find no securable connection between means and ends. Neither business nor ethical philosophy could really happen. By conjuring up an irrational world, Adler suggests reflecting on the meaning of a world without human beings. In that limiting condition, ethics could simply not be a project for anyone. The point of the exercise, however, is not eschatological. Nor is Adler writing science fiction. The point is methodological. The existence of persons, the relevance of an ethical life and the reasonableness of the universe require each other. But while none of these exists of necessity, if any one of these exists all must exist. Adler, the philosopher, overcomes the religionist. He is still the agnostic, still the critical philosopher.

Adler's ethics sometimes seems to depend on a moral sense, a "common consciousness." But are symptomatic responses like resentment, no matter how typical, sufficient for a psychologically sound ethics? Adler misses too much by putting out of bounds the "unconscious," with its moral possibilities and moral dilemmas. And, he ignores a certain playfulness in human beings and thereby impoverishes the moral imagination. The pointless act may be enjoyed without the justification of purpose as in day dreams and games, although, as in inquiry and art, it often turns up something useful. In his seriousness, moreover, the limitations imposed by fortune, by accident, are too easily ignored except as the motive for reconstruction toward the ideal. His absolutist view of marriage and divorce is the extreme case. It may be, however, that under certain conditions what is cannot be reconstructed and that moral action cannot be effective. The moral point then may be consolation and acceptance. But Adler allows little room for the mere mistake and its import. His moral activism cannot leave anything untouched.

Fortunately, moral realism saves Adler from himself. His austerity is corrected by his practical wisdom, as in his acknowledgment of frustration and the "three shadows." For example, he is more successful as a schoolman than would be expected from his apparent rigidity. Volatility is the rule of the classroom, and Adler does not blind himself to it in an anxiety for the ideal. The keen observer of the human condition could have been strait-jacketed by his idealism but he is not. He escapes himself, as it were, because he does not often yield to the temptation to discard or ignore what is but does not fit.

In consequence of his realism, Adler's moral imagination confesses the permanently incomplete. With it, however, he gives a dramatic and active shape to Kant's *noumenon*. It follows that Adler could not hope to be a systematic philosopher on his own philosophic grounds. His story can have no ending, for all the talk of the ideal end. The key for him is ethical experience, which is the outcome of the interaction of worth and value. Ethical experience is thus always caught in the imperfect. Yet it is all we really have, and only a utopian would try to get at ethics apart from it. It follows that process is Adler's ethical style, as in the reciprocal interaction of selves, the emergent character of the ideal, his evolutionary sense of history, his progressive pedagogy and the like.

As method, the moral imagination relies on analogy and metaphor, even where the language seems prosaic and factual.[12] Thus, the distinctiveness of nations is modeled on the distinctiveness of persons. The idea of the talents takes flight from the manifest talent of artist and scientist, joining humanism of the Renaissance, the universalism of the Enlightenment and the passion of Emerson. In all of this, Adler is the advocate of an idealism which

> is thus an interpretation of experience, not the literal truth....It is an imaginative and symbolic rendering of life, illuminating its possibilities rather than describing its actual limitations. Romantic idealists...make no claim to the possession of literal truth....It is the claim of the Idealists that science is not the literal truth either, that all renderings of experience are symbolic interpretations, that all discourse and all knowledge is a metaphor....Idealism, that is, is not science but imagination, poetry and art—and so is science![13]

Fortunately, Adler's rationalism is appearance but not reality. Yet, he does not entirely escape its problematic. It has consequences in Adler's thought which are evident in his effort to convey the idea of uniqueness or distinctiveness as both particular and universal. As a matter of fact, human beings do want personal identity, recognition and meaning in their lives. But, Adler gives these only a morally affirmative reading. He does not admit the possibility that there might be uniquely evil distinctive identities. That would be to embed the irrational in the universe itself. Examples of villainy beyond mere immorality are surely available in human history, and yet Adler seems to deny them their particularity. He does not pay attention to his own attacks on racism, genocide and exploitation.

There might also be identities that emerge from breaking away from relationships. As Guttchen reminds us,

> the monk, the recluse, the Taoist and the Buddhist, the Stoic and Epicurean, in practicing a form of renunciation, might also be understood as seeking a place for themselves and a meaning for their lives.[14]

Moreover, the reciprocal development of selves may not be limited to the influence of good on good and evil on evil. Ethical experience surely teaches that evil may evoke good, or, that good may evoke evil. An act of cruelty, for example, may lead to responses of caring; an act of terror may mobilize the responses of community. Love may produce resentment and care may produce dependence. Since Adler is not a dualist and alternatively does not take evil to be merely the absence of good, his position becomes even more puzzling.

It is not reason alone that leads Adler to diminish the moral force of evil. His views echo his roots in legalism and Hebraism. For Adler, the nature of evil is its commonness, while the nature of sin is its uniqueness. An inveterate punster, Adler no doubt is amused by the twist he thus gives to the notion of originality in the doctrine of original sin. Evil is not original at all. Evil acts are the substance of general prohibitions like those against murder, theft, perjury and the like. To meet this fact of moral history, Adler distinguishes evil from sin. So, the ethical act in the face of evil still remains the "supremely individuated act" and arises precisely because my conscience, my *consciousness* of sin, is my own and not yours.

At the same time, he has a pragmatic intention. None of us can say in advance of the fact what our moral contribution to society will be. Individuality cannot be codified. On the other hand, immorality can be, and this appears, historically, as the legal code and the moral rule. By contrast, seeming rules like "love thy neighbor" are not rules at all but invitations to the expressive personality. Only in experience does such an invitation gain its content, and reveal its individuated features. By referring evil to moral education, as in developing a sense of sin, *i.e.*, the self-consciousness of evil, Adler connects evil with hope. The reconstructive force of sin, unlike the codification of prohibitions, is individuated, is an individual's project. In that way, Adler thinks to avoid moral surrender and moral warfare.

Finally, it is useful to ask whether or not Adler's ethical philosophy is necessary to his philosophy of industrialism. Indeed, he himself seems to raise the question when he advises the readers of *An Ethical Philosophy of Life* that they can omit his technical philosophic discussions of Kant, of worth, of the infinite manifold, and of the supersensible, and still grasp his point. Without his neo-Kantian philosophic apparatus, he might have avoided the rationalism that forced his struggle to cohere fact and idea. Functional internationalism and the vocational reconstruction of democracy can be defended in their own terms, as can Adler's philosophy of culture and education. Adler is surely aware of the problems his idealism raises for his pragmatism and for his appeal to ethical experience. Yet, in the end—as in *The Reconstruction of the Spiritual Ideal*—he does not mute his philosophic effort and in fact embeds his program even more deeply into his philosophy. The reason becomes clear. In a massive and dominant industrial culture, the sacred and the inviolable are all too quickly dismissed as stumbling blocks to success. Mere empiricism reduces to opportunism, and opportunism to exploitation. The ghost that haunts Adler's thought, the idea of worth, remains a specter but it cannot be exorcised.

Excellence

As a philosopher of the moral imagination, Adler's aesthetic and ethic must submit to judgment. In other words, is the ideal Adler proposes worth aiming toward and to what extent is it possible of achievement? The actual interaction of ideal and practice in the present, any present, suggests the burden of Adler's answer. An inclusive society of capable individuals is prerequisite to realizing the potentialities of industrialism. And inclusiveness and industrialism are, in one way or another, the fate of our moment in history. In the historic occasion, however, the premises of the American republic have, in turn, become the suppositions of more and more of the world. The pace and geography of things are changing. The ideal moves ever more quickly from mind to nation to world. Thus, the emergence of the democratic ideal tells us that it is implicit in the moment too.

But the ideal has its competitors. It is not the only way that industrialism can show itself politically and socially. Democracy, like progress, is not inevitable. Human beings can be included in society in many different ways as slaves, as servants, as workers, as clients, as consumers, and the potentialities of industrialism can be realized in many different ways as in technocratic autocracy or newly sophisticated tribalism. Adler's response is that individual, communal and social experience demonstrate the instability and ineffectiveness of democracy's competitors in the modern world. Thus, his ethical philosophy is a life-long argument for democracy's moral and practical desirability. But he does not remain with argument alone.

The question shifts from desirability to possibility, becomes an empirical question, for Adler, an historical question. After all, the moral imagination can conjure up any number of desirable worlds, but it would be irresponsible to disconnect them from the one actual world we do have. The actual, in other words, is self evidently possible and as such is always the beginning point. Hence the persistence of reconstruction is Adler's experiment with the possible.

Reconstruction relies on ethical experience and its potentialities. Thus, both history and biography are evidence that worth is no abstraction and that value is no weakling. For example, Adler makes much of the fact that more than a few persons have lived in the direction of the ideal. This demonstrates that character development is possible.[15] The radical step he takes, however, is to propose that what is evident in some human beings at some time can, with appropriate effort, be taken as possible for all human beings at some other time. He views the progressive move toward excellence as a democratic and not as an aristocratic virtue.

Symptomatically, Adler's earliest effort in 1878, as well as his last effort in 1926, is the school. In it, his democratic radicalism can be tested, learned, taught, corrected, evolved and broadcast. That, after all, is the intention of the progressive notion of the school as model and as community, as both the having of and the preparation for experience. Schools when they attend to their moral mission are thus always suggestive institutions, arenas for the exploration of possibility. As normative institutions in their own right and not mere mechanisms they can be responsive to salient examples, to modeling.

Of course, it takes no great sophistication to fault any particular school for its parochialism. Schools appear within an actual society, are bounded by class and caste values and are limited by accessible resources as well as by the ways in which culture shapes perception itself. Thus, a middle class bias toward the achiever and the technological intellect is typically American. How then can any trans-cultural and trans-temporal claim be made for the school? It is because schools are, when truthful to their intention, always susceptible to further reconstructions. That is the point of schooling, not repetition but re-creation. The model school is not to be imitated but is to inspire. And this is Adler's strategy, to show how schools might be shaped toward a democratic ideal, toward the universally distributed realization of distinctive talents. The effort, of course, runs into opposition and that is precisely the import of education as politics. As he puts it,

> the idea suggested by culture is, to begin with, neutral. It connotes
> growth, faculties capable of development from within, and also an
> advance toward some kind of perfection or excellence.[16]

Adler's agenda is, as usual, both critical and generative. Thus, politics is also education. Adler then sets the school against alternative models, against imperialism with its distinction between civilized and subject nations, against elitism with its distinction between aristocrats and under classes, and against plutocracy with its distinction between those in power and those to be exploited. A democratic society cannot set out to divide its population into the naturally superior and the naturally inferior. A democratic school must exhibit the social connection. Of course, there will be variations of talent and effectiveness. But even these feature in relationships of reciprocity as influences toward mutual development. Given that ethical experience is never entirely ideal and never entirely opportunistic, an imperfect world may in the moment allow for an "aristocracy of talents," as Jefferson put it. But, for the democrat, the development of each individual is the imperative of culture.

Adler is skeptical even of a temporary and open aristocracy. Thus, the critic in him points out that the permanent assignment of any person or class of persons to inferiority is morally indefensible. And any privilege, earned or inherited, tempts to permanence. Ironically, it is also a token of failure. Privilege condemns all individuals to inferiority because the developmental relationship of persons to each other is thereby truncated. The so-called superior, and not just the so-called inferior, is impoverished and harmed. Not least of all, the failure to begin with a premise of a universality of talents cripples the ability of the human being to deal with the three shadows and the pains of experience. These, we recall, never vanish, but they are to be met by action and productivity, by the contribution of each to all. Yet, the message of inferiority is the inability to contribute, to be productive. Life ceases to be tragic and becomes pathetic. Finally, elitism is doubtful because it pretends to a final wisdom about persons. As it were, it freezes the universe in one historic place.

Of course, Adler is not blind to the differences between leaders and followers, the more talented and the less talented. These are, however, moments in personal development and cannot be defended as fixed categories of class or person. In fact, in a highly differentiated industrial society, the door to a pluralism of masteries opens wider and wider. It becomes more and more likely that persons will be masters and apprentices all at once. Specialism may be the problem, but it is also the democratic opportunity. That is why, no doubt, the democratic idea moves so quickly in the modern world.

Excellence, then, is not a claim of fact but a working idea, and it is this that Adler embodies in the school and in schooling. In other words, the school is always experimental, and, in fact, experiment is the mission of all schools in a democratic society. As he put it in commenting on educational reform,

> Their reform movements were in line with the democratic spirit of the age. Pestalozzi extended knowledge downward to an inferior class, made it accessible to the poor; Froebel extended knowledge downward to an inferior age, made it accessible to the child of three. The inclusiveness of their schemes was in line with the prevailing tendency....[17]

Adler, in his own way, lives within the progressive neighborhood. The common thread is evident. For example, Lawrence Cremin notes, "Dewey's definition of democracy was cut from the stuff of American experience....Democracy becomes...a kind of continuing social process of *e pluribus unum*....[18]

Adler is well aware of the anti-progressive and traditional forces that subvert reform. Against these, he urges a sense of possibility and warns,

> take progress as your watchword and your old foe authority will come climbing in at the window....There is a tendency today...to stand for the *status quo* in industry and in politics, to identify the present system with the absolutely correct system, to identify Americanism with the acceptance of the present economic arrangements and to thrust that idea into the schools...indoctrinate the minds of the children...with the idea that things must be left as they are....[19]

Failing the sense of possibility, "the uncommon possibility in the common man," the democratic hypothesis is emptied of hope and becomes but another occasion of resentment.

There is, however, a problematic issue which is hardly noticed by many progressives. The notion of the talents, the Emersonian notion, is essentially benevolent. Talents, as it were, are goods and their development is, therefore, morally desirable. But, the human being can be daemonic, can have a talent for destruction. Can society still be democratic when possibility moves between good and evil? The struggle with that question is the ground on which Adler develops the implications of value and the attribution of worth, the reason why his optimism is based in human choice and not in history's inevitability. In the social setting of family and school, some talents are chosen for development and others are not, and the development itself shapes the ways in which talent is enacted. Except, perhaps, for the genius, the person is not determined in advance of experience by one and only one talent. So to assume the capacity for good in persons is not to assume only the capacity for good. The warfare between worth and value persists everywhere. From that point of view, it could be argued, as James Madison does in "Number 10" of the *Federalist Papers*, that democracy by diversifying, even universalizing, the sources of power guards against the seizure of control. Analogically, checks and balances is a message to the talents as well.

Like other democrats, then, Adler is not sentimental about human beings, even if he proposes potentiality, talent, and reciprocity as

universally distributed capacities, capacities for the ideal. He contrasts
his views with Rousseau,

> [who] struck a note which found its wonderful echo in the breasts of his
> contemporaries...fatigued by an over-wrought and artificial and corrupt
> civilization....The state of Nature is not the ideal state as he pictured it but
> a savage and brutish state. The ideal does not lie behind but in front of
> us....The arts, the sciences, the varied intercourse of man in cities has
> become as necessary to our minds as food is to the body....[20]

Possibility is, then, for Adler an historically complex idea, and its
demonstration is never simply a matter of setting up organizations and
mechanisms. Institutions are in the first instance ideas, and only
derivatively are they embodied as structures. So, it is possible for
organizations to persist while the institutions that once gave them
birth, content and purpose vanish. Intended as examples of the ideal
within any historic occasion, institutions are always at risk. For the
reformer, they are meant to test hypotheticals, in Adler's terms, the
possibility of the ideal. Failure attends them as much as it attends all
else in ethical experience. Yet, the test of possibility is unavoidable.
Institutions, if you will, are philosophically unavoidable. Without
them, the argument for excellence remains merely an argument.

Organized Democracy

Excellence is, as a matter of belief and intention, the human
potentiality. Consequently, the instruments like schools that move us
toward its realization are to be universally distributed. The
development of competence from apprenticeship to mastery is the aim
of a democratic culture in the industrial future. Vocation is the
economic and political form that the process of excellence takes in a
commercial society. Personalized work for everyone, then, is the
essential ideal of a reconstructed democracy. Again, echoes of
Emerson are heard in Adler's thinking. "Self reliance" is re-
conceived to meet the contingencies of an industrial society. That, in
principle, is the solution to Adler's labor question. But, as self
reliance takes on new forms, escaping individualism and turning
instead to mutual relationship, it comes to wear a social costume. It
evolves between person and person as they nurture each other in
reciprocal relationships. By analogy, self reliance is also a
characteristic of groups and develops between collective and collective
in the evolution and control of power. Thus, each vocation brings a

different voice to the public table. The democratic values of equality and fraternity are transformed in response to a new historic moment.

Whatever the changes brought by the industrial occasion, however, the historic continuities of a Puritan past remain. The Puritan virtues, frugality, hard work and productivity are still the signs of grace even where, as with Adler, grace is secularized. The context of this move toward work and worldliness is suggested by a series of historic images. Classicism assumes that character and citizenship derive from political participation, military prowess and aesthetic fittingness. These are surely vocations, but they are radically distinct from the meanings that attach to labor. As vocations, they are, instead, outcomes of a self capable of committing to the *res publica*. The routine work of the world, on the other hand, is external to personality and is assigned by others. So, it is suitable for women, slaves, barbarians and lesser breeds like shop keepers and tradespeople. Alternatively, monasticism embeds work in cosmic necessity and aims its energies at another world. In some quarters, it is regarded, too, as a punishment for the sin of disobedience, the expulsion from Eden. The knight, the courtier and the gentleman assume that mere necessities are to be provided to them by others and inferiors. Life's mission is transcendently grand, and glory not sustenance is its end. For the romantic, escape to the south sea island is a metaphor for the notion that nature provides for us without effort. Finally, in the city slum and factory, work is at best only an economic means, a mere mechanism, and this idea finally spreads its meaning to encompass all work.

In any case, ethical experience tells us that work is perceived not as a blessing but as a necessary evil. And, Adler agrees. As long as work remains drudgery and as long as its performance is determined by the alien other, work is indeed an evil. It does not qualify as vocation and so does not lead toward the ideal. Adler, however, does not turn to leisure and pleasure as the counter-image. We are not to sell our selves away even for a limited time in order to earn the right to be ourselves in another time and place. Idleness and frivolity are as much an evil as wage slavery. Indeed, they generate each other. So, work is to be identified with an ethical culture, with its reconstruction of human energies and relationships as meaningful work, as productive work.

Adler, in his anxiety to solve the problem of the labor question, does very little in his philosophy to account for experiences like appreciation and contemplation. To be sure, he provides for civic "luxuries." His criticism of the slum rests in no small measure on the failure of the tenement to make space for the privacy and quiet necessary to development. And, he insists that the arts are essential to schooling. They are not mere "frills." Yet, the overwhelming impression is a certain earnestness and austerity. And this, in turn, suggests that the personality formation he proposes lacks a certain balance.

The emphasis on productivity, the act of working as such, also underplays the nature of the product. After all, mastery entails doing something very well. No doubt, Adler simply assumes a world of attractive and useful objects without attending to criteria or meaning. Yet, in the hands of too many progressives the outcome of this kind of neglect is an uncritical acceptance of the shoddy and the amateurish as equal in value to the crafted and skilled. The fate of the arts in some progressive schools and the interpretation of criticism as damaging to the ego are instances of this neglect. Adler, of course, does not take that path, but his lack of a well developed aesthetic invites it. He does connect the talent to the actual production and not just to productivity. In his life-cycle portrait of human development, he makes a distinction between master and novice, a distinction of skill. But it is not enough.

Adler enters the problem of the product in a different way and with a different intention. His agenda is moral development. This is his priority. From that point of departure, to turn the product into an object valuable in itself makes the value of productivity dependent on some external achievement and to that extent not dependent on the achievement of an ethical personality. When, as in commercial society, the product, like the process, is alienated, then this dependency becomes doubly problematic. So it is that Adler tends to slight the richness of experience for the sake of ethical experience. He does not deal with the status of the aesthetic object as such. Yet, it surely is not simply an object of value, not simply a thing to be used or destroyed.

Perhaps, then, the categories of value and worth are ethically insufficient, just as object and person may be ontologically insufficient. Products like a well crafted table or a great painting may have an integrity of their own and, indeed, may convey it without reference to a producer at all. The artist may be unknown and in some instances unknowable. A culture may value anonymity or collectivity, as in folk art and some religious art. For Adler, however, art and craft are always instrumental to the ideal and always signed— connected to personality—even where the signature has been scratched out by time or circumstance. Symptomatic of the consequences of his narrowed attention, he remarks over and over again in conversation and in public utterance that he intends to write a "book on friendship." But despite a prolific output in speech in writing, he never gets to it.

Clearly Adler believes that industrial society is amenable to reconstruction. In fact, he is more radical than that. He denies the moral seriousness of anyone who would think to start with a clean slate. For him, that is a sign in the reformer of the worst kind of utopianism and in the philosopher of the worst kind of academicism. The moral issue is how to go about reconstruction in the actual and only society we have. In response, Adler develops the idea of organized democracy with its echoes of the American Revolution, the division of labor and the marriage of science and technology. With vocational groups as the units of the reconstructed state, political economy is, as it were, to be resurrected against the diseases of specialism and mechanism. The American ideal is to be brought up to date. But, as Adler confesses, his vocationalism is not fully developed. In fact, it is problematic not just because it lacks attention to the richness of experience but in the face of ethical experience itself.

For example, everyone is to find a place in a vocational group, and no one is to be left out. Thus, Adler extends the idea of vocation to women. But there are other members of society where that extension is hardly possible. Unlike women, the student has only a brief and temporary membership in what is only a proto-vocation. Of course, there will always be a population of students, but the group's membership is of necessity volatile and shifting. It lacks, therefore, the condition of stage development and persistence through biography that makes representation possible. Adler struggles with this problem but never solves it. Thus, he calls the Fieldston plan "pre-vocational" and urges the university to be "vocational." But the mood of preparation and temporariness remains. For the student as student, the passage from novice to mastery ends in departure and not in right abdication. The student achieves vocation only when he or she is transformed into something else and shifts moral location. In fact, the perpetual student is a token of failure. And while learning is a life-long activity, the very universality of its distribution negates the specificity of the vocation. At the same time, the young man or woman, despite a lack of vocation, has public obligations like paying taxes or military service. But, his or her representation is unprovided for. That, in an organized democracy, is impermissible.

A similar puzzle arises with the emergence of a population of retired persons. Of course, Adler could not foresee late twentieth century industrial demographics. Yet, by his own criterion, his ideas must meet the test of experience. Perhaps, it is possible to interpret "emeritus" status as the penultimate moment of all vocations, as the first step into the process of right abdication. But political and economic interests are at stake for the retired as such, and this would seem to be independent of the prior vocational situation. As with students in life's beginnings, there is here a transformation at the other end of life. Location shifts away from workplace to some unaccounted for living space.

In this setting, representation is not the only problematic of the new demography. On Adler's grounds, personality continues to develop until death and requires vocation for its means. But, the old are radically excluded from both society and personality in some significant ways and only partially empowered as continuing but decreasingly active members of former vocations. The young may model vocation in the school but, although important and even indispensable, this is play-acting and not participation. The organized state is thus an uncompleted notion.

This inadequacy is further illustrated by the problem of human rights in an organized democracy. On his own grounds, Adler cannot appeal to a general sense of equity, nor can he rely on natural law, although at times he tries to do both.

> Self defense has generally meant standing up for one's own rights....The only possible way to defend ourselves...is to bear in mind that our right is an organ in the organism of rights....It is the duty of the individual to defend himself....It would be immoral in him to practice a policy of non-resistance. He should not only protect the humanity that resides in his own person but should also protect the humanity in the person of the aggressor. He should prevent...[the] latter from perpetrating a crime and save him from losing to that extent his character as a human being....[21]

Rights, then, are neither given nor inherent but need to be continuously asserted in the act of demanding them. But, in an organized democracy, that demand appears through the vocation. Self defense, in other words, requires the presence of all parties. Representation cannot be abdicated. So, for the person without vocational membership, the student or the retired person, rights have no ground and cease to exist. And, of course, that is neither Adler's intention nor his point of view.

In a similar way, there are sources of identity that it would seem cannot be reduced to vocational membership. Race, geography and ethnicity are part of our ethical experience too. Adler certainly understands the depth of these. Thus, he knows out of painful and direct encounter, the problems of the German-American during World

War I. He is passionate on behalf of minorities and people of color after the Civil War and clearly sees imperialism as a racist activity. He appreciates the affirmative contributions of race and nation to identity as in his almost gentle references to his Jewish roots and as in his relationship to his father. Indeed, he interprets nationality as the contribution of a collective talent to the orchestration of the human race itself. Yet, organized democracy has no place for these. Race, geography and ethnicity are not vocations.

In short, Adler has, without fully appreciating its implications, defined democracy in terms of economic functions, even where he attempts to transform these into ethical and spiritual functions. He is caught in the mood of his time.

> The period which [Charles] Beard called the American counter-Reformation (c. 1890-1914) was acutely conscious of the primacy of the economic factor in modern life. [James Harvey] Robinson traced the origins of the new history to *The Holy Family* of Marx and Engels; Beard made his reputation with his *Economic Interpretation of the Constitution of the United States*. Dewey and Tufts located the most urgent ethical problems of 1908 in economics; [Justice] Holmes looked to the lawyer trained in economics as the man of the future, anticipating in 1897 the emergence of Louis Brandeis's mode of legal thinking....[22]

Vocations are inevitably afflicted by problems of value. Thus, organicism is as ideal always imperfect. Vocations will exhibit selfishness, exploitation and insularity in their relationships with other vocations and in internal hierarchies of power and interest. The evolution of the labor union, surely well known to Adler, is its illustration. Adler's ideal state thus has serious difficulties as political science. But, like Plato's *Republic*, it finds its usefulness as political and economic criticism. A new politics, for example, is suggested by the inadequacies of "one man, one vote," the political reading of equality and fraternity.

> The emphasis of brotherhood...is the sign of an honorable reaction against the unjust discriminations...in the social system....The emphasis on likeness is a rebound against the unfair, untenable distinctions that have been made between man and man. The real unlikenesses, however...are...the very condition and opportunity of the higher development of the race...The over-stressing of fraternity...is a formidable menace to the moral progress of society....[23]

Adler's organized democracy makes sense as a criticism of the first century of the American Republic. It takes us to the question of a realistic reconstruction of representation, but it does not take us all the way. It makes visible the democratic possibilities of industrialism.

Reform or Reconstruction

Adler's philosophy of reconstruction is a criticism, too, of "mere" reform. "We are drifting now...mere experimentalism without an ulterior end...." The criticism, however, is also self criticism, for Adler too is a reformer. And the reformer has his reply, which Adler cannot help but echo out of his own experience. Confronted by a confusion of claims on human energies, the reformer often has all he or she can do to come up with temporary working ideas. The ideal end may be clear, but the mediating goals often are not. In fact, it is not unusual for these to wind up in contradiction. And Adler surely learns this lesson when, for example, he establishes a printer's cooperative, only to find that it falls apart when wages rise after the industry comes through depression. His schools, retrospectively, seem to evolve in a clear direction toward the ideal. In practice, the record, as it should be, reflects trial and error, temporary successes and temporary failures. Not least of all, reform reflects the politics of value, where alliances of interest come into being and pass away. And again, Adler learns this well as a member of New York's Tenement House Commission and as a labor arbitrator.

Adler's philosophy is surely directed outward to others in the progressive neighborhood, but it emerges from an internal dialogue, a reflection on the complexities of his own ethical experience. "The better," he comments, "is often the enemy of the best." Reason is on the side of the *telos*. But Adler knows the temptations and the urgencies of the moment. As a realist, he must respond to the event. As a reformer, then, he is never secure or secured. His is an uncomfortable reform.

Adler's social idealism has its uses for the human being caught in the "blooming, buzzing confusion" of experience, particularly industrial and commercial experience. So, while Adler allows for flexibility in "the means by which the goal is to be reached," he confesses its danger to the ideal from within experience itself. The ideal then serves as a point of judgment in the present. If, then, he sounds utterly certain, his assertiveness can be read as a form of philosophic therapy.

Anxious to "treat chance relations as if they were necessary relations," Adler exhibits the need for coherence and control.

Inevitably, he underplays the role of fortune and leaves almost no room for spontaneity. As a reformer, he gives ample evidence of the ability to seize the moment. As a thinker, he remains something of the rationalist but, as with reform, it is an uncomfortable rationalism. Nothing ever quite goes according to plan. Every reformer and every institution builder knows that. And yet, without a plan, an end in view, it is not even possible to know if things have gone wrong or gone right. Mere movement, mere change, becomes reform's meaning.

So, finally, Adler is an instrumentalist and, even the ideal is an instrument.

> [T]he word, "instrumental" is of decisive importance....To be a cheerful world builder, to take an active and whole-hearted interest in the improvement of material conditions, in political reforms, in the embellishment of earthly life...and at the same time to keep the spiritual end in view as the supreme end....The answer...is to be found in the words "partial success and frustration." The finite...[is] means to the highest end....the inevitable defeat of our effort...serves to implant in us the conviction of the reality of the infinite ethical ideal....[24]

Vision and reality are at play with each other

> an ideal is an idea or mental picture of something that ought to be. The ideal condemns the actual. There would be no need of an ideal if the actual were what it ought to be...but...(the) ideal appreciates the actual in so far as the actual conditions lend themselves to betterment. There could be no ideal if the actual were not capable of being made what it ought to be....[25]

Given the relationship of ideal and actual, of worth and value, Adler warns the reformer—and himself as reformer—of the moral and practical dangers of separation. There are no "deserving poor" waiting for the beneficence of the wise, the rich and the powerful. In an imperfect society, everyone is afflicted in one way or another, everyone is needy, including the reformer. The issue is not charity but community.

> My neighbor has need of me; there is something as yet hid in him which I must help to make manifest; and also I have need of my neighbor. There is something in me...for the revelation of which I depend on him.[26]

Reform has, therefore a democratic basis. Presumptions of superiority are its failure.

Human destiny is a shared destiny among distinctive equals who in their conduct create each other as moral beings. Thus, the reformer need not be a slum dweller or "on the line" in order to be in a community with the poor or the factory worker. The reformer, on Adler's grounds, is concerned with changing the person of the poor, the laborer, or what have you, so that he or she will have the capacity to do for himself or for herself. Reform is then an ethical relationship and not a manipulative activity. Of course, the conditions of life are not to be ignored, but they are only ancillary to the work of reform. Adler's ideal is again a criticism not just of "this reform or that" but of wrongful attention.

Ultimately, Adler believes that no person can save anyone but himself or herself. Yet, this cannot be done by oneself. The task is "to make social institutions just by the instrumentality of better men and to make men better by the instrumentality of a more justly ordered society...and to hold the two ends jointly...."[27] Radically different experiences, say of race or class or gender, are for Adler the source of moral growth and not the justification of moral isolation.

Clearly, Adler's philosophy of distinctiveness permits a responsible social role for the privileged, the successful and the talented. Reconstruction presumes that society and all of its members are in need of reform. It presumes, too, that they know it or can come to know it. *Noblesse oblige* is transformed into democratic responsibility.

Philosophy or Mere Moralism

What then, finally, is Adler's contribution and his place in the history of ideas? An effective preacher and educator, he seems unable to escape an imitative metaphysics and the temptations of mere moralism. Certainly, he has his convictions, and he is dedicated to convincing others. He uses story, argument, authority, appeals to self interest and to a sense of fairness—all the devices of pulpit rhetoric—to achieve his ends. But his passion never deteriorates into sentimentality, and his ideas, whatever their source, take an original turn.

Adler is of that generation of great platform speakers which, long before the mass media, brought the latest news of scholarship and the issues of the day to a popular audience. Effective as he is, he is also well aware of the dangers of the spoken word and the dramatic performance, noting that

mere exhortation is of very limited utility....The consequence...is that
either a purely nominal and hypocritical assent is secured by the preacher,
or in case the words are taken seriously to heart, the consequence will be
"to send men into the bush" to use Emerson's words....[28]

Adler walks that pathway of the "career of philosophy" illustrated by Spinoza's "*amor intellectualis dei*," the integrating of activity, inquiry, passion and ideal. In a sense, then, he seems to fit in with the existential and even the post-modern, a strange place for a neo-Kantian idealist and a Victorian. No doubt, he sounds alien to the modern Anglo-Saxon philosophic ear. The dangers of wishful thinking and unintended bias inhere in this weaving together of self and reflection too. And yet, mere objectivity, whatever that really comes down to, is as problematic. If the one tends to blind us to the inadequacy of our ideas, the other easily makes our ideas trivial.

Often unconfessed, there is always a good deal of self-doubt in philosophy and among philosophers. Lacking a precise subject matter, philosophy takes the entire range of experience and cosmos for its concern and so is often either pretentious or irrelevant. Aware of this, frustrated and impotent, philosophy retreats to the specific, almost any specific, that seems to promise an identifiable territory to it. So, the attempt to determine if Adler is a philosopher runs into the blockades of the moment, of fad and style. Perhaps then, we can do no better than to accept William James' realism. Philosophy is what those who call themselves philosophers do. Of course, he put it more felicitously.

A philosophy is the expression of a man's intimate character....If we take
the whole history of philosophy, the systems reduce to a few main types
which...are just so many visions, modes of feeling the whole push and
seeing the whole drift of life, forced on one by one's total character and
experience and on the whole *preferred*—there is no other truthful word—as
one's best working attitude.[29]

Philosophic problems shift, not because they are solved but because they cease to interest someone. And philosophic problems return as experience puts them before us in a new way. The question about Adler, then, is one of whether or not he is interesting beyond the historic moment.

Adler moves creatively from his Kantian base to problems of reflective practice in an industrial society. But, just because of his idealism and its language, this move is often obscured. For that reason, I have tried to show how ideal and practice together lead to his notions of vocation, culture and democracy. Indeed, Dewey might well be referring to Adler when he writes,

> There is...a close connection between the vital problems of philosophy and the conditions manifested in living culture....if philosophy is fundamentally a criticism which brings to light these problems and gives them clarity...and if...philosophy can do no more than point the road intelligent action must take—then the greatest service any particular philosophical theory can render is to sharpen and deepen the sense of these problems....[30]

In fact, Adler moves from ethical formalism and rationalism to pragmatism whenever he attends to industrial society, *i. e.*, whenever he works with his own agenda and not someone else's. His roots and his language as much as his philosophy, however, prevent him from identification with his pragmatist colleagues like James and Dewey. Both of them, by the way, were known to him and he to them—James as a sometime member of the Philadelphia Ethical Society and summer neighbor in the Adirondacks, Dewey as a fellow member of the Columbia faculty. Consequently, Adler remains philosophically isolated and at the same time pragmatism does not benefit from his idealistic critique. Naturalism does need *telos* which, in turn, needs the benefit of biology. Adler's organic imagery and his rejection of mechanism confesses the need on both sides.

Adler is sensitive to the speculative features of his thought. And despite temperament, he recognizes that it is a developing project with all of the contradictions and false starts that attend development. As he remarks at the Plymouth Summer School,

> If the effects are manifestly disastrous, then the presumption is that the ethicist was mistaken...and if so-called moral demands are made which...the world could not live by...the moralist...has substituted some airy fancy of his own for the utterance of moral truth or...he has distorted and misread the testimony of the moral sense....our views...will be considerably cleared up...by compelling...those who advocate them to prove that they are workable....[31]

With a commitment to practice, he announces his allegiance to the pragmatic criterion without saying so. Adequacy is not the outcome of mind but of world and the world is unforgiving. Thus, Adler "strongly opposed the complacency and optimism of the Hegelian idealists....His shrewd and realistic appraisal of 'empirical man'...enabled him to protest...just those aspects of...liberal idealistic humanism which now seem most tarnished and faded...."[32]

It is hard to say whether Adler's achievement is a religious philosophy or a philosophic religion. In any event, these two interests inescapably shape his career in thought and in practice. Their unity explains his passion and his realism. And it is precisely in that integration, given life through utterance, institution and reform, that I locate his relevance for a society which so easily fragments everything in the name of clarity and efficiency.

I began this essay with Adler's existential response to the pains of experience. "Out of the depths into which it has fallen, humanity cries today for help...." Thus, Adler begins his last text, *The Reconstruction of the Spiritual Ideal*. And that finally suggests his significance for us and the reasons why that significance has escaped us. In a sense, the personal has only recently been re-discovered as a philosophically legitimate theme. Ironically, despite Adler's paternalism, Victorianism and his attitude toward marriage and divorce, his message forecasts much that arises today under the inspiration of feminism. With it, connection, individuation and caring are brought together as a criticism of rationalism and objectivity. Adler's voice, strangely, sounds the same note and, more to the point, is in the same spirit.

A philosopher of the moral imagination, Adler sets the personal in a tragic background. The ideal tells us that failure is inevitably our lot. Yet, purposeful action and achievement are not foreclosed. Between despair and hope is the work of philosophy. But, thought always has its reasons in the world as it is. Insisting on this practicalism, however, Adler leaves the philosopher unsatisfied. There is just too much passion for objectivity. He leaves the religionist unsatisfied too. There is too much realism for commitment. And he leaves the reformer unsatisfied. There is too much thinking for action. And yet, it is precisely this catalogue of dissatisfactions that exhibit the strength of Adler's effort. He is, finally, an example of his own philosophy of relationship, his announced mission against specialism and mechanism. Biography, then, is verification, but that tells us that verification is always a personal obligation. Second-hand truths and truths at a distance will not do. Distinctiveness is an epistemological and a moral duty.

Notes

[1] In a letter Horace Friess wrote to me in 1970, he said:

> His fellow philosophers saw in Adler's systematic effort some points of originality, but most a derivative outline—a noble edifice, no doubt, but filled out more by moral counsel, programs and critiques than by analyses. However, it gained in stimulus through this method, it did not fully enough close in on questions they were venturing to answer.

[2] Felix Adler, "The Religious Education of Children," undated (probably before 1895), pp. 2–4.

[3] By way of reminder, I think of Dewey on education, the Existentialists on the subjective, the painful and the irrational in experience, economists like John Kenneth Galbraith on countervailing power. I suggest, too, Adler's insights into the needs of a reconstructed representative government, and the hints about affirmative action and automation and a living wage.

[4] It is helpful to compare Adler with Morris Raphael Cohen of New York's City College. Cohen faced anti-Semitism in a way that Adler never knew. As a middle-European Jew and immigrant, Cohen never had the security of Adler's background. His career in a secular institution, however, offered a more open intellectual environment. Finally, Cohen's work on modern technical problems of philosophy, *e. g.*, logic and philosophy of science, was more at home in the climate of the day than Adler's neo-Kantian idealism. See Leonora Cohen Rosenfeld, *Portrait of a Philosopher: Morris R. Cohen in Life and Letters*, New York, 1962. For Cohen's relationship to the Ethical Culture Societies, see Radest, *Common Ground.*

[5] For the most explicit development of Adler's Kantianism, see *An Ethical Philosophy of Life*, Part II.

[6] *Nichomachean Ethics*, Book I, Chapter 3, in *The Basic Works of Aristotle*, Richard Mckeon, editor, New York, Random House, 1941, p. 936.

[7] John Herman Randall, Jr., "The Churches and the Liberal Tradition," *The Annals of the American Academy of Political and Social Science*, Volume 256, March, 1948, p. 149.

[8] Felix Adler, "The Freedom of Ethical Fellowship," *The International Journal of Ethics*, Volume I, 1891, p. 23.

[9] Felix Adler, "Leadership in the Ethical Movement (A New Vocation)," address, April 24, 1898, p. 15.

[10] Adler, *Reconstruction*, pp. 192–193.

[11] Felix Adler, "The Relation of the Moral Ideal to Reality," *International Journal of Ethics*, Volume XXI, 1911, p. 18.

[12] For a useful and interesting discussion of this theme, see Dorothy M.

Emmett, *The Nature of Metaphysical Thinking*, New York, Macmillan, 1953.

[13] John Herman Randall, Jr., *The Career of Philosophy*, Volume 2, New York, Columbia University Press, 1965, p. 203.

[14] Guttchen, *Felix Adler*, p. 23.

[15] On this point, see Felix Adler, *The Moral Instruction of Children*, New York, D. Appleton and Company, 1898.

[16] Felix Adler, "Philosophy Club Notes for the Oxford Lectures on Education," 1923, p. 15.

[17] Felix Adler, "The New View of Childhood," address, March 24, 1895, pp. 8–9.

[18] Lawrence A. Cremin , *The Transformation of the School*, New York, Vintage Books, 1961, pp.121–122.

[19] Felix Adler, "The Foundation of a Better Social Order as Laid in Education," address, January 29, 1922, pp. 3–4.

[20] Adler, "The New View of Childhood," p. 5.

[21] Adler, *The World Crisis*, pp. 52–53.

[22] White, *Social Thought*, pp. 76–77.

[23] Adler, *Reconstruction*, pp. 132–133.

[24] Adler, *An Ethical Philosophy*, pp. 268–269.

[25] Adler, *The World Crisis*, pp. 85–86.

[26] Felix Adler, "The Spiritual Basis of Reconstruction," January 1919, p. 2.

[27] Felix Adler, "A New Type of Religious Leader," *Ethical Addresses*, Volume XVII, 1910, p. 219.

[28] Adler, "First Lecture," Plymouth, p. 4.

[29] William James, *A Pluralistic Universe*, New York, Longmans Green, 1909, pp. 20–21.

[30] *The Philosophy of John Dewey*, Paul Arthur Schilpp, editor, Evanston, Ill., Northwestern University Press, 1939, p. 607.

[31] Adler, "Second Lecture," Plymouth, pp. 10–11.

[32] Randall, *Career of Philosophy*, Volume 2, p. 160.

BIBLIOGRAPHY

Adler, Felix, *An Ethical Philosophy of Life*, New York, D. Appleton-Century Company, 1918.

— *Creed and Deed*, New York, G. P. Putnam's Sons, 1877.

— *Incompatibility in Marriage*, New York, D. Appleton and Company, 1930.

— *The Essentials of Spirituality*, New York, James Pott and Company, 1905.

— *The Moral Instruction of Children*, New York, D. Appleton and Company, 1892.

— *The Reconstruction of the Spiritual Ideal*, New York, D. Appleton and Company, 1924.

— *The Religion of Duty*, New York, McClure, Philips and Company, 1905.

— *The World Crisis and its Meaning*, New York, D. Appleton and Company, 1916.

Bacon, Samuel Frederick, *An Evaluation of the Philosophy and Pedagogy of Ethical Culture*, Washington, DC, Catholic University, 1933.

Baker, Carlos, *Emerson Among the Eccentrics*, New York, Viking, 1996.

Black, Algernon D., *Without Burnt Offerings*, New York, Viking, 1974.

Blau, Joseph L., *Men and Movements in American Philosophy*, New York, Prentice Hall, 1952.

Bridges, Horace J., editor, *Aspects of Ethical Religion: Essays in Honor of Felix Adler on the Fiftieth Anniversary of his Founding of the Ethical Movement, 1876*, New York, American Ethical Union, 1926.

Broad, C. D., *Five Types of Ethical Theory*, New York, Harcourt Brace, 1930.

Cremin, Lawrence A., *The Transformation of the School (Progressivism in American Education 1876–1957)*, New York, Vintage Books, 1961.

Dewey, John, *A Common Faith*, New Haven, Yale University Press, 1934.

— *Intelligence in the Modern World*, Joseph Ratner, editor, New York, Modern Library, 1939.

— *Reconstruction in Philosophy*, New York, Henry Holt, 1920.

— *The Philosophy of John Dewey*, Paul Arthur Schilpp, editor, Evanston, Northwestern University Press, 1939.

— *The School and Society*, in *Dewey on Education*, Martin S. Dworkin, editor, New York, Teacher's College, 1959.

Durkheim, Emile, *The Division of Labor in Society* (1893), translated by George Simpson, New York, The Free Press, 1964.

Emerson, Ralph Waldo, *Selected Essays*, Larzer Ziff, editor, New York, Penguin Books, 1982.

Fairfield, Roy, editor, *Humanizing the Workplace*, Buffalo, New York, Prometheus Press, 1974.

Flower, Elizabeth G. and Murphy, Michael, *A History of Philosophy in America*, 2 volumes, New York, Capricorn Books, 1977.

Friedmann, Georges, *Industrial Society (The Emergence of the Human Problems of Automation)*, Harold L. Sheppard, editor, New York, The Free Press, 1955.

Friess, Horace L., *Felix Adler and Ethical Culture, Memories and Studies*, Fannia Weingartner, editor, New York, Columbia University Press, 1981.

— *Our Part in This World (Interpretations by Felix Adler)*, New York, King's Crown Press, 1946.

Frothingham, O. B., *Religion of Humanity*, New York, G. P. Putnam's Sons, 1877.

Guttchen, Robert S., *Felix Adler*, New York, Twayne Publishers, 1974.

Hornback, James F., *The Philosophic Sources and Sanctions of the Founders of Ethical Culture*, New York, unpublished dissertation, Columbia University, 1983.

James, William, *Essays on Faith and Morals*, New York, Meridian Books, 1962.

— *Varieties of Religious Experience*, New York, Macmillan, 1961.

Jefferson, Thomas, *The Portable Thomas Jefferson*, Merrill D. Peterson, editor, New York, Viking Penguin, 1975.

Kant, Immanuel, *Critique of Practical Reason*, translated by Lewis W. Beck, Chicago, University of Chicago Press, 1949.

— *On Education*, translated by Annette Churton, Ann Arbor, University of Michigan Press, 1960.

— *Religion within the Limits of Reason Alone*, translated by Theodore M. Greene and Hoyt H. Hudson, New York, Harper and Brothers, 1960.

— *The Fundamental Principles of the Metaphysics of Ethics*, translated by Otto Manthy-Zorn, New York, Appleton-Century Company, 1938.

Kraut, Benny, *From Reform Judaism to Ethical Culture: The Religious Evolution of Felix Adler*, Cincinnati, Hebrew Union College Press, 1979.

Lamont, Corlis, *The Philosophy of Humanism*, New York, Ungar, 1982.

Mead, George Herbert, *Selected Writings*, Andrew J. Reck, editor, New York, Library of Liberal Arts, 1964.

Miller, Perry, *The American Transcendentalists*, New York, Doubleday, 1957.

Nathanson, Jerome, *John Dewey: The Reconstruction of the Democratic Life*, New York, Ungar, 1967.

Olds, Mason, *Religious Humanism in America*, Washington, DC, University Press of America, 1978.

Persons, Stow, *Free Religion*, New Haven, Yale University Press, 1947.

Radest, Howard B., *Humanism with a Human Face: Intimacy and the Enlightenment*, Westport, Praeger Publishers, 1996.

— *The Devil and Secular Humanism*, New York, Praeger Publishers, 1990.

— *Toward Common Ground (The Story of the Ethical Societies in the United States)*, New York, Ungar, 1969.

Randall, John Herman Jr., *The Career of Philosophy*, two volumes, New York, Columbia University Press, 1965.

Riis, Jacob A., *The Making of an American*, New York, Macmillan Company, 1901.

Roth, Robert J., S.J., *American Religious Philosophy*, New York, Harcourt, Brace and World, 1967.

Turner, James, *Without God, without Creed*, Baltimore, Johns Hopkins University Press, 1985.

Schneider, Herbert W., *A History of American Philosophy*, New York, Columbia University Press, 1946.

White, Morton, *Social Thought in America (The Revolt Against Formalism)*, Boston, Beacon Press, 1957.

Wright, Conrad, *A Stream of Light*, Boston, Unitarian Universalist Association, 1975.

Note: Felix Adler's addresses and papers together with related texts and materials can be found in the following:

Archive, The New York Society for Ethical Culture

Rare Book and Manuscript Library, Columbia University Libraries

INDEX

*A*merican Liberal Religious Thought

This series is devoted to monographs and collections of essays that explore historically and develop constructively the tradition of American liberal religious thought in the context of its ongoing relations with other forms of thought, especially those of American philosophy. Themes pertinent to the "Chicago School" of theology and to naturalism in American theology and philosophy figure prominently in the religious liberalism focused on in these volumes. The sponsor of the series is the Highlands Institute for American Religious Thought, a community of productive scholars with diverse religious and philosophical perspectives that has its headquarters in Highlands, North Carolina.

Peter Lang Publishing
Acquisitions Department
275 Seventh Ave., 28th Floor
New York, NY 10001